PEDDAR ZASKQ
...in this moment

An Introduction to the
Ancient Science of Dhunami

© Copyright 2009, 2016, 2020 Dhunami

ISBN # 978-0-615-21482-5
DHUNAMI.guru

This book is dedicated with Divine Love to the Dhunami Masters, and to every individual who seeks Divine Spirit and Truth.

INTRODUCTION

Contained herein are the timeless, universal teachings that Sri Paul Twitchell presented to the world. You will find the book to be informative and enlightening whether you are familiar with his writings or entirely unaware of his works.

Sri Paul was the modern day founder of Eckankar...an individual path for spiritual liberation within one's lifetime. After his translation (death), Sri Darwin Gross was introduced as his successor; he was in charge of continuing to present and teach his material and expand upon it.

However, in the fall of 1983, a coup was instigated by the board of directors, led by the man who was in training to succeed Sri Darwin. Eckankar was taken over and Sri Darwin was ousted. While this man's intentions were well known to the Hierarchy of Dhunami Masters, each individual must be free to choose his or her own path on the road to Self-Mastery. Shortly thereafter, Paul's original writings were edited and vibrationally diluted for the purposes of converting Eckankar into a religion.

This event was nothing new. When reviewing the course of spiritual history on the direct path to Sugmad (God), the necessity of periodically changing the outer name becomes clear. Whether by appropriation or by the imposition of a state religion causing this way of life to go underground, the Living Master always remains flexible and adaptive for his survival and therefore the perpetuation of the path in the lower worlds.

The Living Dhunami Master of the Time is the genuine source of spiritual Truth. He must remain in the human form until the next man is ready to accept the spiritual mantle of responsibility. Purity and continuity of lineage is the key to preserving the vitality of Dhunami's unaltered vibrational message whose purpose is to serve you, the authentic seeker of Truth.

It is for these reasons that Sri Paul Twitchell (whose spiritual name is Peddar Zaskq) has dictated this book. Herein, he clearly re-states the original teachings, now called the Ancient Science of Dhunami, while addressing many issues that individuals are misinformed about, due to the dilution of his writings.

How is this possible, you may ask? Well, that question brings us to the book's subtitle, in this moment. Peddar Zaskq, or Peddaji as he is called in the familiar, hasn't gone anywhere; he is here, now. There is life beyond death, and there is contact with beings beyond death, especially the Masters of the Dhunami Order. As the Designated Mahanta, Peddaji works with and through me to fulfill our mutual spiritual duties of sustaining the direct path to Sugmad. He will continue in this role for several hundred years.

Developing the ability to see and hear both the inner form of the Living Dhunami Master and others among this ancient Hierarchy is what is taught and practiced by those who choose this way of life. By accepting the Master's help with opening your inner hearing and seeing faculties, you are provided with recurring opportunities to prove all things to yourself. You gradually become the 'Knower' by experience, rather than a curious seeker or faithful believer.

The book you are about to read carries with it a gradually increasing vibration with the turn of each page. The flow of Divine Dhun Spirit you'll experience is from the pure realms of Sugmad whose vibration is placed into the content. By using Peddaji's name in conjunction with the spiritual exercises of Dhunami you'll be able to have inner experiences with this great Dhunami Master.

For those who know these teachings and were initiated either under Sri Paul Twitchell or Sri Darwin Gross, a familiarity will be sensed, not only for Paul's style but also for that feeling of Divine Love. It is the gift, it is your answer, and it is always given even before you ask. If you will rely upon that feeling while trusting that it contains all the answers you're seeking, then the spiritual experiences necessary to prove the truth of what is being presented will certainly follow.

By the use of the daily spiritual exercises outlined in this book you will become increasingly aware of the other worlds of existence described herein. You'll become aware of the presence, guidance and Divine Love of the Inner Master which is the way the Living Dhunami Master contacts, guides and protects the individual Soul who is ready. These exchanges or encounters typically occur in the dream state in the beginning while later on it is a matter of actual seeing and hearing with the spiritual eyes and ears; the counterparts of the human senses.

If you will open your heart and let Divine Love enter in without compromise while these pages are experienced, that unmistakable feeling, that eternal answer, the gift of the Master, will be recognized, realized and accepted...in this moment.

May the Blessings Be!

Paulji

Sri Paul Marché
The 973rd Living Dhunami Master

Chapter One
April 7, 2008

Past Lives
Spiritual Desire

This is a strange feeling for me, being the one dictating, because I've been the one being dictated to for so long. This may come as a surprise to some of you, especially those of you who have been with these teachings for a short amount of time, but one soon comes to realize that in these teachings anything is possible.

It's very subtle – this flow of Divine Spirit – and sometimes we will not recognize that what is being said to us is from Spirit. We think it is our conscience, or intuition. Learning to open our spiritual ears and listen is a great task to accomplish, but it is one that we must accomplish.

The purpose of this book is many fold. This chapter is to help people understand how they can and will have past life experiences, and the importance of these experiences. There is a great deal that can be learned from these experiences, and once learned or known, can be applied to our present life situation to improve it, and make things easier on ourselves. It is a way of learning inwardly that which we are required to apply to our outer lives, which is essential in this lifetime for our spiritual growth and progress.

Many times the individual will have glimpses into a past life during the dream state, and doesn't realize that the Master is there and is showing the person this past lifetime for a reason. However, it is up to the individual to request to see more about this particular lifetime, and to desire to understand its bearing on the present lifetime.

This is how the Master works. He points something out to you, or points you in a certain direction, but it is up to you to make the choice of whether or not you are ready for it, and whether or not you want to explore it, whatever it is that the Master has pointed to.

I want to take up the subject of desire for a moment. The student must have a desire to unfold spiritually in the first place, which causes the Master or Masters working with this particular individual to point to something, and begin directing the person. Desire is nothing more than some feeling and some attention.

Therefore, if we put a certain amount of feeling, be it love, gratitude, or some other positive emotion, and combine it with our attention placed on the Inner Master, or the Light and Sound, this individual who does this will soon begin to have experiences during their contemplative exercises, and during sleep, and the Master will begin to work with the individual during these times to help the individual progress spiritually.

There must be some feeling attached or used with the attention, or the seeker is not going to be very successful in his spiritual endeavors. This has been written many times before, but it needs to be said again.

Past lives can often be a subject of great importance to the individual, but most people don't even think twice about them. They think that whatever's in the past should stay there, and to an extent, these individuals are right. Some students are afraid to see their past lives, or have feelings of shame or guilt associated with their past lives.

What the individual does not understand is two things: First, the Master is not showing you this life to make you afraid or to evoke any type of emotion in the seeker whatsoever. For this purpose the Master will often show events leading up to, but not the specific event that would evoke such feelings in the seeker.

For example, if I were being shown how I died in my previous lifetime, and seeing this particular event would upset me, and cause me to get emotional, then I would be shown the events leading up to, but not my actual death.

Second, the point I want to make here is that the Master only shows you what is needed for your spiritual growth and development. This usually pertains to something like a karmic situation with someone, a situation where our ego was out of control, or perhaps a lifetime where we were betrayed, causing us to have little to no trust in people in our present lifetime.

The individual will only be shown a piece or pieces of something that could hold him back in the area of spiritual unfoldment. We can always request more information, or if we want to know how something was done or made, we can ask. People ask all the time how the pyramids were built. That question should be aimed at Gopal Das, who was the Living Dhunami Master in Egypt during that time period in history. He'll tell you how it was done, among other things, but he won't show you your lifetime there – that is up to another Master – the one who initiated you. I think I've made myself clear on this part of the subject of past lives.

Past lives are often difficult for the individual to understand, and sometimes it may be necessary to write them down and look at them at a later date. One should always remember to record the feelings experienced during the past life dream or the contemplation. Often the feelings we feel will tell us more about what we have to learn from the experience than the experience or images themselves will tell us or show us.

Not every person on this path or in these teachings will have past life experiences, because not everyone has something in a past life that needs to be worked out this lifetime. Or perhaps the individual will not be shown because he or she has already worked past whatever problem or issue that was in their past life or lives. Sometimes the individual will have a past life dream or experience and not remember it. Some of us don't have to see it and feel it consciously for it to be worked out in our other bodies.

Past lives are just one area that the individual can learn from, and gain a greater understanding of his own behavior and position in this present life.

We don't do Akashic readings, or past life readings, for a number of reasons anymore. The first being that there aren't many people who want to take up this task, as it is no small feat. The second is because it is very time consuming for both the reader and the one who has requested the reading. Another reason is that the individual requesting the reading may not be fully ready to hear about his or her past lives, and to recognize what needs to be learned from them, meaning that which is pertinent to his spiritual development at the present time.

The Eck-Vidya book is a wonderful tool for an individual who wants to learn more about themselves, their lives, and the cycles of men and nations. But it is only meant to be a starting place, for it does not contain any specific individual suggestions or guidance. Only the Inner Master can do that for us.

If one is to understand his innermost workings, his automatic reactions caused by triggers in the subconscious, he must do so through the spiritual exercises and through the dream state with the Master. This of course requires the complete faith of the individual in the Inner Master, as well as a level of surrender, because the Master cannot point out what is needed, or what is there causing problems if we are blocking him, if we are unreceptive to the guidance, or if we think we already know.

Hence, complete surrender and faith in the Master is required to have any level of success or growth in the area of past lives, and the chela will soon recognize that the same is true in many other areas of spiritual concern, as well as our outer lives which are guided and taken care of like our inner lives, as long as we surrender to IT (Divine Spirit) and are receptive of IT.

The guidance that the Inner Master gives to the chela, in all areas of spiritual growth including past lives, is given because of the Master's pure and impersonal love for the seeker. The Master asks little in return for his love, attention, and wisdom. For this reason and this reason alone, it is up to the chela to return the Master's love, to have gratitude for the Master, and to sincerely try to adopt the lessons and techniques he gives us. The Master soon learns who is sincere in their spiritual goals and who is not, and he will wait patiently for anyone who is not ready to learn the secret teachings. He does not care who takes up the study of Dhunami, but he will not waste time on anyone who is not honest with themselves and is only interested in psychic or material gain.

Once the Master has established that the chela truly has Self-realization and/or God-realization as his goal and is willing to follow the Master and his instructions, the Master will make sure that the chela progresses as fast as his consciousness will allow. This is why some students have greater success with the teachings and perhaps have experiences quicker than others – it all depends on where the individual is working from, and how quickly they can surrender themselves to the Inner Master.

Chapter Two
April 8th, 2008

Inner and Outer Master
Duties of the Chela
Importance of the Spiritual Exercises

D own through history man has always looked to an outside source for answers concerning his spiritual unfoldment. This has caused most of man's problems and will continue to do so until man realizes that he can only look to the outside for so long. And by so long I mean a very short amount of time. While we all need the outer Master to set our feet upon the path of Dhunami, and continue to give us our initiations and perhaps some wisdom in the written form, this is as far as it goes. Man must then turn to the inner temple, go inward to make any real progress in the spiritual worlds.

Unless man has some sort of idea of who to look to, or who will guide him on the inner, he can wander around the inner planes, even causing himself more trouble, getting into more karmic conditions and getting caught up in areas that don't do us any good. The Master guides us on both the inner and the outer planes, meaning he helps us on the physical with his lectures, writings, and maybe some music or poetry. This helps us both inwardly and on the outer because it all trickles down, you see.

The things that we learn, our spiritual lessons, can help us in our physical lives in a number of ways. If we are more honest, not only with ourselves but with those around us, that will greatly improve our outer physical lives, but it's something that needs to be worked out and developed in the spiritual areas first, in many cases. Another area is karmic conditions. When those finally get worked out, which the Master always helps with on the inner, this usually improves our day to day lives, and our physical relationships with those around us. There are many, many examples of this, but I think you are beginning to see the point.

It matters not what the Living Dhunami Master of the Time looks like, what his past occupations or actions were. And people should not be looking to the personality of the Master because that's not going to help you in any area of unfoldment, physical or spiritual. Any individual who wishes to have any sort of success in the spiritual worlds has to look at the Master as just that – nothing more. He's not here to be friends with us, or to impress us with any of his traits or talents, but only to help us unfold spiritually.

The Master needs plenty of good clear channels that he and the Order of Dhunami Masters can work through. Now, I know some people will think, 'they're Masters, why do they need the help?' Well, it's partly because there's a vast amount of work to be done, not just on the physical plane but on the lower planes, as well as on some of the higher ones, and all of the universes. Most people forget that there are plenty of other planets populated with plenty of people who are also seeking spiritual upliftment. Now the Master also needs plenty of clear open vehicles or channels because people like to talk to other people. I can't talk to every single person I would like to, not just because of time, but because sometimes their awareness or their state of consciousness will not allow me to on the inner.

That's when the Masters will work with an individual who is able to talk to a person, especially someone interested in the teachings. Sometimes it takes a certain person's experience, and when telling that story a light bulb comes on in another person's head, or they suddenly have an understanding that they couldn't grasp before. This is why the Master needs so many pure channels, and why the channels he has must be active as far as giving introductory talks, or holding book discussion or discourse classes. And all of this takes very little time and effort on the chela's part; to do the talks and classes.

Now I want to say that if you're giving these talks or classes, and you want to share an experience, an inner experience, and you're not sure if you should, then don't and I mean don't! You'll know if you're supposed to share it or not. Myself, or DapRen, or Rebazar Tarzs or whoever you're working with at the time will give you a little nudge, or a push, if it's something we feel you should share with a group or a particular person. However, you will only get this nudge if you are open to it. Some people are so afraid they're going to say the wrong thing, or share an experience that they shouldn't that they don't want to say anything at all. And that's alright too.

Sometimes that person in the class or in the audience at the lecture will pick it up, inwardly that is, and you don't have to say a word. Darwin wrote about this, that the realization can come later, maybe a week, maybe a month, but it will come if we want it to, no matter what vehicle or channel it must travel.

I want to say that those of you that are giving introductory talks or holding classes, and even just those of you who are putting up posters or handing out brochures, that you are not only helping other Souls, but you're helping yourself as well. These actions are all working off bad karma, as well as storing up good karma. The person who has been waiting and waiting for that next step, but it doesn't seem to be coming, should try one of the above mentioned methods of outer work. That individual will often have the realization or unfoldment he's been waiting for rather swiftly after doing some service in the name of the Sugmad.

Now often times people will say they don't have the time, or the resources, or don't like to talk in front of other people, that's just fine too. There are other ways of being a vehicle on this physical plane. Sometimes just smiling at someone is enough to catch their attention or interest, and get them thinking, 'why is he so happy?' So you see, we can involve ourselves in these outer works as little or as much as we want to, but no matter how much we do, it's always going to come back to us spiritually. It's always going to have an effect on our spiritual unfoldment and growth.

The next thing I want to talk about tonight is sincerity, and I know I touched on this a little last night. If the chela is going to do some outer work, he or she must be sincere about it, not just doing it for their own development, but because they really want to make the message of Dhunami available, and the key word is available. Holding a class simply because you think it is going to get you your next initiation, well that's not going to help most of the people in the class very much, and it's certainly not going to help you. Rebazar Tarzs told me, and I believe I put it in the <u>Stranger by the River</u> book, that to give without ever once thinking about the reward is when we truly start to live, and by this I mean live on the inner planes, where we should all be striving to live. Placing our attention at the Temple Within is the best way to start, but again, that's just to start.

Many people think that the outer service that they do, or time that they give, makes up for neglecting or dropping their inner work, or their contemplative exercises to be specific. These people could not be more mistaken. If we're not going within daily, if we're not giving our time and attention to the Masters, even if just for a short amount of time, then we are not going to be very effective in our attempts either on the physical with classes or lectures, or on the inner with our spiritual growth. Darwin used to say one half hour was all it took, but really if a person did not have even that much time, that would still be alright. Any amount of attention the chela gives to the inner worlds, or the Inner Master is time extremely well spent, and the chela will come to feel this and know this.

This is where the sincere chela can get into a bit of trouble, so to speak, by putting off the contemplative exercises or thinking that they'll make up for it another time, or do it later. And usually later turns into later, which turns into much later, and soon the seeker has lost the habit or discipline built by the spiritual exercises, as well as the inner growth that comes with them. Even when we think nothing is happening it's usually because we have not taken the time to develop the spiritual eyes and ears to know what is happening during these contemplative states. However, it does not take long once the chela makes a sincere and honest effort towards these contemplative exercises.

Often the Masters will know that you have little time for your exercises, or that you have trouble focusing or sitting still for a period of time, due to any number of reasons. The Masters will work with you in the dream state, as long as you are putting forth some sort of effort, or you have the desire to have the experiences. Once certain things are gained in the dream state, consciously or not, the chela will find it easier to sit still longer, concentrate better, and may even have realized something that they wish to contemplate on, something they would like to know more about, to have answered within themselves.

Now every time the chela asks for something the Master hears it, especially if it is done in the contemplative state. Sometimes the Master works to get the chela unfolded or his consciousness open to the point where he has what he has asked for. Other times the Master works hard to see that the chela doesn't get what they ask for, because if it came to the chela, or was realized by the chela, it would do much more harm than good. This is why sometimes it is better to simply ask for guidance, or spiritual growth, rather than a specific ability or physical or material object.

Know that the Master is working for your spiritual unfoldment, for that is all he is concerned with. If you desire a better job, or a different house or car, it is up to you. You will be guided every step of the way, but that old saying that God helps those who help themselves is true, in a way. All this is stating is that we must do the work, meaning apply for jobs or work a little overtime if we want a different house, but also have faith in the Master that he will guide you to the right place to apply for that job, or the right neighborhood for that house.

Many things are important on this path of Dhunami: faith, honesty, sincerity, initiative, but the most important is keeping up with the daily spiritual contemplative exercises. I believe it is the best thing we can do for our spiritual growth, and if we put that foot forward, and we show a little desire, the Masters are going to notice, they are going to listen, and they're going to give us every possible thing we can handle, as fast as we can handle it.

Chapter Three
April 9th, 2008

Steps to Self-Mastery
Trust and Mistrust
Entities and Spiritual Protection

I f the individual desires Self-realization, or discovery, there are a number of things one can do to achieve this. The first step of course is finding the Godman on this physical plane, and taking up his course of study. The next step then is to be initiated under this Godman, for he will see to it that you attain the goal which you set for yourself. The next step is to faithfully practice the spiritual exercises and contemplative exercises that the Living Dhunami Master or Godman sets for the individual.

This will be done in the books, discourses, and even at the Temple Within. The techniques that the student receives at the Temple Within with the Master should be applied and used primarily, because even though it seems like just a word, or a different seating position, it is specially tailored for that individual who received it. Now I want all of you to understand that just because you don't seem to get special instruction or don't seem to have any special words given to you, this does not mean the Master isn't working with you.

Some people need or want that extra push – that word given to them in contemplation. Some people need it, but others do not. If you are one of those that don't have a certain word told to you, you are just as blessed as the person who does.

Do not ever feel like the Masters are neglecting you, or that some people are getting more attention or special attention, because this is just not true, and by having this attitude and putting forth this idea, you are sending a negative thought pattern to the Master, and he may have to withdraw his presence. Anytime we are having negative thoughts concerning the Master or the teachings, we are only hurting ourselves.

I am not talking here about questioning, that is very healthy, and is encouraged. What I am talking about is thinking that the Master is unfair, or isn't acting right, or is fake or lying. It is alright to question and wonder, 'is this particular teacher or Master or path right for me?'

Usually when the seeker is not having any experiences, or any type of special instruction on the inner it is because of one of two things. The first being that the student is doing fine, and doesn't need any sort of conscious specific guidance. The second is that this individual is not open to the guidance or direction of the Living Dhunami Master of the Time, because of their ego, or because they doubt that anything can or will happen to them in their spiritual exercises or contemplative state.

How do we tell the difference; how do we know or discover which one we are? Ask. It really is as simple as that. Sit quietly; try to clear your mind of all thoughts. If you need an image to keep things from popping into the mind, use any that you like, as long as it is a Spiritual Master, a blue or white light, or Jesus, or some type of Saint. You must ask clearly if you are open, or if you are closed, or ask if you are progressing, or simply if there's any guidance or special instruction for you at this time. Then let it go.

Now, it may take a little while for the answer to come through, and by this I mean a few days or a few weeks. The important thing to remember here is if we don't get the answer right away, or at that particular time, to continue with our exercises, or contemplations, because that is the only place the answer is going to come. The Masters can't give it to us when we're walking around or having dinner usually, or playing with our children. We must put our time, energy, attention, and feeling on the Master or the Light or the teachings if we expect to get anything.

This does require patience, but you'll find that the minute you stop haggling over it, being bothered by it or letting it hold your thoughts, that's about when you'll get what you were looking for.

Now I would like to discuss the issue of trust. If one has a lack of trust in the Master, or in people in general, then that individual's spiritual progress will only be so far, then this mistrust must be remedied. The only way or rather the best way to end mistrust is to realize that if people are dishonest with us, they are only harming themselves. Just like if we are dishonest, we feel the brunt of that, or the karma that comes with it, that is our burden to pay, if we lie.

The chela soon learns that if he or she leaves everything up to the Master, and follows his guidance, that our whole lives, both the inner and the outer are taken care of. Sometimes all we need is to see this once or twice; that the Master has worked something out for us, and immediately we trust the Master. Other times it takes more experiences. The Master will attempt to give the chela all the experiences and time he needs to learn trust, because it is such an important quality to have. However, some chelas will refuse to see the positive in a situation, or will think it should have turned out better, and this is a very detrimental attitude to have for oneself.

Trusting the Master means we as individuals trust everyone else too, to an extent. This does not mean we open our house to strangers, or we don't lock our cars. This means that we trust the Master to handle whatever situation comes into our lives. If someone tells you they're going to do something for you, and they don't, it doesn't matter, because if it needs to be done, it will be done.

Darwin Gross always said he was the biggest doubter, that he questioned everything, but he ended up very spiritually advanced because he learned to trust right away, because he would question, and he would get an answer, and he would believe it.

Sometimes we will get away with it. The Master will let us get away with not trusting, or with some other folly or behavior that we should be trying to lose, but usually only for a short amount of time. Then they let you know 'hey so and so, it's time to drop this.' If you're open to it, and you want to be rid of it, you will be very quickly. Those Beings working as Masters and with the Masters on the inner planes are very powerful Beings, and they can only use that power for our spiritual development. If on the other hand you're holding onto it, be it mistrust or another similar issue, and you're grasping it like a blanket, they won't pull it away from you, but don't expect much else either. They can only do so much, basically that which we ask of them. Anything further is a violation of spiritual law.

Anytime that you think there's a Being in your midst or in your psychic area that is not there for your benefit, you challenge it in the name of the Sugmad. If it is not a good situation, that entity will disappear.

As a chela on this path, the student receives an amount of spiritual protection that cannot be measured or accurately expressed in words. People don't really understand what kind of entities there are on these inner planes, especially the lower ones. It's been talked about to some degree, but perhaps more on the subject will have to be explained in the future. I don't talk about this to scare anyone, or make anyone think they have to join this path and get the protection or they're going to be in serious trouble – I'm not saying that at all. What I am trying to say here is that there are plenty of entities on these other planes that can attack you on the inner, and even influence you here in the physical.

This type of situation is a very sad and terrible one for the individual involved, who many times does not even realize what is taking place.

There are so many ways to protect ourselves and our space from these entities, that there's no reason to ever be afraid or to give them a second thought. This will all have to be explained later, but for now, the individual can take some comfort in the fact that just being a chela and practicing the presence of the Master and the spiritual exercises, one need never know of any entities or black magicians.

Until the time that the individual takes up the path of Dhunami, he is at a vulnerable position, since he is mostly unaware of himself as Soul, and has not explored and developed his own consciousness. Only by surrendering to the Inner Master can we truly have security and freedom.

Chapter Four

April 10th, 2008

Self-Surrender
Light is Knowledge
Purpose of the Sound Current
Spiritual Techniques

Today I would like to take up the topic of surrender. This sounds very simple, and yet it is probably the most difficult and complex thing one ever has to do in their lifetime here on this physical plane. True surrender means that we give up every aspect of ourselves, including our minds and egos, which are separate from our personality, and yet we retain our individuality.

This may seem like a big paradox to most people, but you will find the higher you go in these teachings and the more you progress towards God, the more we find paradoxes. Once we understand these paradoxes, we have realized them and adopted them or overcome them, then we can continue to progress spiritually. One does not overcome or accept or learn these paradoxes through the mind. In fact, that is a big misconception, as well as a trap. To allow the mind to haggle over these paradoxes, these subjects like surrender without losing identity, I am that I am, and yet I am no-thing, if we allow the mind to get a hold of these, we are pulled down into the mental world, and we can get stuck there.

Now, it's okay to use the mind in our daily lives. It is there so that we can make a living for ourselves, and so that we can do our day to day responsibilities. However, this is not where we want to spend most of our time, as far as awareness or consciousness goes. Because we want to get above the mental plane, into the pure positive God worlds. Once we get there, and we begin to really surrender some of these lesser things, including the vanity and attachment to them, that's when we finally come to understand that we don't need them.

I spoke before about trusting the Master and turning everything over to him, and it's only after we do this that we realize things work out better that way. Only through surrender can we be truly efficient and only through surrender of everything, can and will we have everything we need.

So, since we have established that we need to surrender, how do we go about doing that? Again, it really is as simple as asking, and doing the contemplative exercises and spiritual exercises. Darwin always wrote to say, in our daily surrendering 'I, of myself, can do nothing.' And he was really on to something there. If we can say this to ourselves every day, then soon we begin to feel it, and once that happens, we think about it a little, but then we give up thinking about it, and when that happens, then we have realized it. Realizing these points for ourselves is the only way to reach the Kingdom of Heaven now, in this lifetime, and there's no reason for each and every one of us not to.

Sometimes we will wonder if we are worthy, or we doubt whether or not we can do it. We must surrender all of these doubts and insecurities as well; because what good do they do us? We should never allow anything consciously to hold us back from that which is ours, that which we already have if we would but realize it.

Tonight I would like to discuss a topic that has always been a joy for me, and that is knowledge. Not the kind we get from books, or college, or any of these outer negative means or vehicles of knowledge. The only true knowledge is the Light that comes when we are having a contemplative exercise or spiritual exercise. When I first started in these teachings, I didn't quite understand what the Light was or why I was seeing it.

I know this has happened to many of you as well, throughout your lives, before you got in these teachings, maybe it even led you or helped you to find these teachings. The wisdom that we get on the inner from this Light that we see; it can hardly be read or found in any book on this physical plane. Some of the books in these teachings come close, especially the discourses, but the Light we see on the inner is such a unique kind of Light, because it imparts wisdom or knowledge, whichever word you like to use, without words. Now I don't know of anything else that can do that. Even pictures have to be broken down or translated into words before we can understand what is being communicated.

So the Light is a truly special occurrence, when we see it, which can be on the inner and on the outer once we have developed ourselves enough and allowed enough Light into our awareness. The wisdom that we get from this Light is automatically absorbed since there are no words, and is thus immediately effective. This Light gives us knowledge of God, the Masters, the other planes, the inner planes, I mean, and can even give us knowledge about ourselves, our situations, and those around us.

Now don't misinterpret what I'm saying here. The Light gives us knowledge, and very directly but not in the way we would expect. The Light goes right to our subconscious and sometimes our lower bodies and it will help to clear out negative thought patterns which help us to realize the positive ones. Now I don't mean that you'll see this Light on the inner and all of a sudden you'll jump up with a new piece of information, or knowingness. It has to work on us for a while, and then some time later, often days or weeks later, we can have a realization that helps us or brings us one step closer in our quest for spiritual development and discovery. This is part of why it is so essential that the chela faithfully practices the spiritual exercises and contemplative exercises, because there is no other way to gain what we gain in these states when we're getting the Light.

The other aspect that develops with the spiritual exercises and the contemplative exercises is the Sound, which is even more useful or beneficial to us than the Light is, but in a bit of a different way. The Sound carries with it the higher vibrations of the inner worlds that we are trying to reach. By hearing this Sound, it 1) allows us to measure where we are now in our spiritual development, and 2) helps to raise our vibrations so we can take the next step up in our spiritual lives.

The Sound carries away most of the negativity, negative thoughts, feelings or emotions, and in this way it helps to purify us of our imperfections. When anyone hears the Sound, they are truly blessed, and they should know and be happy that they are making real spiritual progress towards their goal of Self-realization or discovery, or God-realization.

Those of you who do not see the Light and hear the Sound yet, there could be a number of explanations for that. Usually it is something within ourselves, some thought or notion that is blocking it. This could be the thoughts that the spiritual exercises are not going to work, having no faith in the teachings or in the Master, and not having an open mind. Or it could be negative thoughts, such as those about ourselves, those around us, or our present living situations. We should never try to have a contemplative exercise when we are angry because it will do us no good.

People don't often want to look critically at themselves when something doesn't work. Instead, they like to think it just doesn't work. It's like when we are building something, a piece of furniture or a model car, and we don't really pay attention to the directions, we just glance over them. And then we think we're finished putting it together, but we have pieces left over, or it doesn't look or work quite right.

Well, it's the same case here. Sometimes we need to spend a little more time on that project, and be aware and conscious of what we are doing, and it's the same with the spiritual and contemplative exercises.

There's no need to worry if we're not having experiences right away, or we can't see or hear anything right away, because if there's something within ourselves that is blocking these things, a feeling of some sort, by chanting or singing the word HU, or any of the other words in this teaching, or the name of the Master, or any of the Masters, IT's already working to remove whatever block is in place, keeping us from realizing and recognizing the Light and Sound.

The wonderful thing about this is that those words can, and should be chanted or sung constantly, whether we are at work, at play, alone, or with our families, because this chanting or singing can be done silently, within ourselves, or it can be done out loud. I always liked to sing out loud, even when I'm not alone, but some people are shy and need to work up to this. I'm not saying to neglect your duties, or take your mind off of your work, if it is a type of work that requires you to focus or use your mind.

However, this chanting or singing helps ourselves in a number of ways. This goes for both those new to the teachings and those who have been with the teachings for a number of years. It keeps your attention on Spirit or God, allows us to be guided by It, allows It to reach us easier. It helps purify us and raise our vibrations, it keeps negative thoughts and feelings away and out of our minds, which is a superb aid when we are working on the five passions of the mind, which I will state quickly for those of you who are unfamiliar with them: Anger, Attachment, Greed, Lust and Vanity, with the most treacherous one not necessarily the first. Anyway, it helps us to focus our attention, which aids us in our spiritual exercises and contemplative exercises. It removes mental blocks and attitudes, as well as feelings that keep us from realizing our goals, and finally it cultivates in us a discipline that is needed increasingly as we develop spiritually.

Whenever you feel a negative thought or feeling coming on, especially about another person, chant or sing the sacred word for God, HU, and those thoughts and feelings will flee from your consciousness so fast, you may not even notice that they're gone, and more importantly, that they are not coming back. This is especially important for two reasons: 1) we do not want to create any new karma or karmic conditions for ourselves by our own thoughts and feelings, and 2) keeping a balanced and positive outlook is the only way we will ever reach Self-realization and God-realization in this lifetime. We will never get there by back-biting or hating our fellowman, and so this technique of chanting or singing should be valued, and well-used by us all.

Chapter Five

April 11, 2008

Inner and Outer Guidance
The Chela's Relationship with the Master
Getting and Giving Divine Love

L et's get to work. Today I want to discuss the subject of inner guidance. It is not everyday that the Masters begin to speak to us on the inner, it takes a certain amount of unfoldment and effort on our part, as well as an attitude of being receptive. Now we can get into one of two situations here, being overly what some people call confident, but really it is being the extreme opposite of humble. This is where we think we know what's good for us, what our general direction in physical and spiritual affairs should be, and when we think we can recognize our own faults so to speak, or obstacles, is a better word.

I think some people call it being strong-willed, or hard-headed. My own mother was that way, to an extent, and so I learned at an early age that I probably could not see these traits or behaviors in myself which needed adjusting.

The other area we can get into here is one of self-degradation, where we feel like our whole Being needs to change, meaning we don't recognize any of the good traits within ourselves. Also, when we have this sort of outlook, we will think or feel that we're not worthy of the Master, and his attention and guidance, or that we of ourselves cannot hear it or know it.

This is a very terrible area for one to get into, and it really is such a shame to see individuals damn themselves, because there is no reason for it, ever! I want each and every person to realize themselves as a part of the Divine, a Spark of Spirit, as it has been said, and really understand that they, themselves, are IT. This has been written about and spoken about as the I Am principle, and people, when you hear about this or read about it, you need to take it seriously and literally because It is!

That's another thing. Many people think that what is written in my books, especially <u>Stranger by the River</u>, as well as DapRen's material, is metaphorical, or is prose, or is using symbology. This is not true at all, everything that is written by a Dhunami Master or is dictated by him as in this case is literal and is meant to be taken that way. We've seen too many times in history where a spiritually developed Being has tried to reach the masses, tried to speak to them to communicate God and Heaven, and how to reach it. Too often these Spiritual Beings do use allegories, or symbols thinking that this is the way to get the masses to understand what they are saying.

Instead, they end up confusing their followers and those who look at their words, and cause them to become even more lost, or put them further back on their journey to find realization. The Masters on this path, no matter how they reach you; through their own writings, dictations, letters, or on the inner, listen closely as to what they say, because they are giving it to you straight, and they mean every word of it.

If you are receiving some sort of information on the inner, it is for your benefit, and that alone. The Masters of this Order of Dhunami are not able to speak of themselves, or say or do things with selfish intent, or for their own benefit or popularity. It is against spiritual law. Every single one of these Masters has offered himself to the people as a way to lift them up, as a way for them to reach Self and God-re-alization and that is all. He does not list his accomplishments, or try to convince you that you need to follow him, nor does he condemn you if you don't. Because in these teachings and in dealing with the Masters of this great Dhunami Order, it is all about Divine Love.

All these Masters, including myself, can do, all we want to do, is give Divine Love. Because once you feel that love, once you are open to it and let it touch your heart, you will never again know loneliness and unrest. Once you feel this Divine Love, you begin to want more and more of It, and pretty soon you are filled with It, and then you begin to want to give It out as well. It is contagious, and we can all help in giving out the Divine Love to the people who are looking for It, seeking It, and yearning for It.

I think I'd like to talk a bit more about the individual's relationship with the Master. This is a subject that has been talked about often, but still many people don't quite understand the delicacy and the exchange that occurs there. Rebazar Tarzs talked about this, I think it was in Dialogues with the Master, which is basically the same format and idea as this book, in that it was dictated to me by Rebazar Tarzs, the great Tibetan Master.

In Dialogues with the Master, Rebazar Tarzs states that the Master needs the love of his chelas to continue his work, just as we need the Master's love to be uplifted into the Divine Current. Now I am not talking here about the physical love, or what man thinks is love, but the pure Divine Love that we only feel when we're consciously in the presence of the Masters, or when we are doing our spiritual or contemplative exercises, and when we are in the higher worlds.

Now this Divine Love is the sustaining force, as well as the creative force, and can also be a destructive force, should the need be. It is all there really is, and there exists enough of this Divine Love within us to fulfill all of our own needs, as well as help those around us to unfold. All we really need is this Divine Love in our lives, and It cares for everything we might trouble over.

However, most of us are not aware of the love lying dormant within ourselves, and many do not take the time or energy to uncover it. Most people would rather latch onto someone who gives their love freely, without any effort required. This is why so many people bounce from one religion to the next, continually searching for what seems to be just beyond their reach. They are actually searching for that which is within themselves, this Divine Love, and the Masters help us to uncover It a little at a time, as fast as our consciousness will allow.

Part of it is developing the 360° viewpoint which helps us in every aspect of our inner and outer lives. The key to all of this, and all of life, really, is Divine Love, but so few people in the world recognize this. Some people recognize it in the Living Dhunami Master, but then we have to ask ourselves 'how do we give out our love like the Master?' I'm not saying here that we should try to be like the Master, or try to act like the Master, but one soon learns in Dhunami that the more Divine Love you allow to flow through you, unimpeded, and without directing it, your life and the lives of those you come into contact with are better – so much better, richer, and fuller, and we are so much more awakened. There are hardly words to describe the transformation that takes place.

Every now and then someone comes forth and asks how they can get more of this love in their lives. Well, I think Rebazar Tarzs said in Stranger by the River; in order to get love you must give love. Now as I just stated earlier, we are all filled with enough of this love to sustain us for a very long time, as what man thinks of as time here on Earth. All we have to do is uncover this love within ourselves, and then let it flow because love is a fluid substance, it is like water, you can't hold onto it, and you can't even direct it or tell it where to go – if you try, it still goes where it pleases.

So one must learn to reach the love within himself. How do we do that? should be the next question. Some people think that having Divine Love and giving Divine Love is all about service in the sense of community service, or helping the poor or the elderly. Well, I have a few things to say about that. First is that no one ever got into Heaven based on good deeds. Good deeds or actions do help accumulate good karma, but as long as we are undeveloped or unaware of ourselves as Soul we will have to come back to reap that karma.

Second is that who is to say that community service is really service? Some people need a push, not a helping hand or a handout. On the same note, we all have to make our own way in this world, and there is always something we can contribute. I think those individuals that give of their time and coin are well meaning individuals, and some programs are very useful, especially the Veterans Affairs, but we in these teachings are not here to save the world and we'll soon realize if we go out into the world with that attitude, that most people don't want to be saved.

The next thing is that we can only truly help people when we have helped ourselves, and when we fully understand and have realized ourselves. The only way to do this is through the Living Dhunami Master and the spiritual exercises of Dhunami. This is what develops and brings out the Divine Love within ourselves, and this is the only thing we have or have need of in any of the planes of existence, physical or spiritual.

You'll find that when this love begins to be uncovered, and starts to come out, our whole outlook on life has changed and we no longer recognize who we used to be.

Chapter Six
April 12, 2008

Initiations and Responsibilities
Communicating Through the Heart

N ow I know some of you are wondering a little bit about initiations. The initiation can only be given by the Godman, the Living Dhunami Master of the Time, or through one of his open, clear vehicles, if it's an initiation for the lower planes, or those before and including the Soul plane.

Before the individual is initiated by the Living Dhunami Master of the Time, he or she should have studied for a period of about two years, should be a discourse subscriber, and should be having some sort of experience during the spiritual or contemplative exercises. This is of course between the chela and the Master, but I want to make sure people aren't jumping into anything.

One big thing that people don't realize is that there is a level of responsibility that comes with each and every initiation, each step of the way. It becomes greater and greater with each step the chela takes, and this responsibility is in many areas: it is to the Living Dhunami Master of the Time, it is on the inner, and it is on the outer as well, which many people seem to forget.

The responsibility to the Living Dhunami Master of the Time is to faithfully practice the spiritual and contemplative exercises, to continue to be an open and active vehicle for this Master, even after he has translated from this physical plane, and to his writings and works that he produced while he was on this physical plane.

The responsibility on the inner is to begin to understand and realize what we are doing consciously there, and to help, eventually, with some of the work. At first, when the chela is relatively new to the teachings or is in his first few initiations, this responsibility on the inner is to rely on the inner, to get our answers there, and begin to get our knowledge there primarily as opposed to out here on this physical plane. We must become conscious of what we are doing in the inner, including in the dream state, for many reasons. Sometimes we may need to call on the Master during the dream state, and this is part of our responsibility to develop that ability within ourselves.

As the chela progresses on the spiritual path and becomes aware of himself as Soul, it is now time for the chela to begin to work with the Masters on the inner as far as helping them with their work. This can be in many areas and this is often how one decides if he would like to become a Saint in these teachings, or if he would like to continue on the path as it stands. The chela can help in any area, be it with new students, with animals, with children, learning to heal or write, or play some instrument, or learning to draw. All of this can and will be developed if we want it to.

The responsibility the chela has to the Master on the outer is the one that is neglected the most. This can be fulfilled in a number of ways, and the chela should not feel any sort of resentment or pushing on the subject at all. This responsibility doesn't mean that we have to give introductory talks, or book classes, or discourse classes, although these are all very needed and encouraged and is always paid back on the inner. Other ways of helping on the outer, such as putting out a brochure, leaving a poster, or simply helping someone else set up a class or talk. Now, if you would rather work on something else, due to the increase in technology, there are many other things that can be done, such as writing emails, designing posters, web pages, preserving the Dhunami books, videos, mine and Darwin's tapes as well as keeping records of events and pictures. So many things can be done in front of a computer now, which is considered working on the outer, and one doesn't even need to leave the house or speak to anyone if they prefer not to.

This needs to be restated again and again, that we have responsibilities. If we do not want these responsibilities then we can spend more time in the lower worlds and even on the Soul Plane, until the time is right for us to progress. If one thinks that he can shirk his responsibilities or avoid them, he's got another thing coming. Every chela in these teachings must earn what he gets, and I think the work the individual needs to do or can do is a more than fair trade for the spiritual growth and guidance given from the Master. Every time the chela calls on the Master he has to answer, if he has initiated that chela he has to answer. This is why it has been stated that the Master chooses his chelas very carefully.

Now, sometimes the Master can only see the potential in the chela, and has trouble looking at the things he may haggle over or hassle with. Other times the chela changes so rapidly, in either direction, that the Master does not recognize the chela, or even the potential in him that was there to begin with. What I am saying here is that we can step away from the Master, or we can ignore the Master, but he cannot ignore us, or step away from us. This is why I urge the seeker to be sure he or she wants to step onto this path of Dhunami. If we are careful and really think about what we want to get out of these teachings and out of life in general, then we can possibly make the greatest and most beneficial step of our lives by becoming a student. However, if we are just looking for psychic gains or material gains, we had best turn elsewhere.

The individual taking a look at these teachings can easily get overwhelmed. It is best to go slow with the information here and take our time. Some of you will pick up a book and know immediately that this is the path for you, and that you have probably been on this path before in a past life. For some of you it may take years before you are even sure you want to read a discourse. We have more time than any man can possibly imagine or comprehend. Darwin spoke of this many times, and urged it of his chelas and those reading his books. We never rush on this path, although we are taken as swiftly as we can go through the lower worlds, if Self-realization is truly our goal. I know that I myself many times have had to step back for a moment and get back into balance before trying to progress any further.

That is the biggest thing the Master wants for us, next to having and giving Divine Love, is for us to learn on our own how to recognize when we are out of balance, learn how to get back into balance, and try to prevent ourselves from getting out of balance again. In these teachings, we want to take it a step at a time, and a moment at a time, and if there is something that we don't like happening, or something we don't like being said, we can walk away from it, and suddenly we are in the next moment again, and we're not going to worry about or think about what happened back there.

Too many of us spend time thinking about the past, feeling what we felt in the past and having harsh feelings about the past and what we might have done. I am talking here about guilt, shame, and damning one's self for no reason. If the Masters cannot turn their back on the chela, and they cannot have anything but love for the chela, why should we feel differently about ourselves? We have no reason to feel guilty about anything, and certainly no reason to be upset with ourselves, or look down on ourselves, or feel we do not deserve what the Master has to show us and give us.

Every time we have a negative thought about ourselves, we are causing problems for ourselves, and setting up negative conditions for ourselves that we do not need for any reason and should not have to go through. Stop being so hard on yourselves! If you are doing something wrong you will know it and the Masters will point it out to you, or get you to understand in some way.

The Masters communicate to the chela through the heart. When you get a warm feeling, and a good feeling when you see the Master, that is what is happening there, he is touching your heart. If you're about to do something, and you get a feeling that you shouldn't do it, that's the Master speaking to your heart. This is why the Master is able to reach so many people at so many levels. Where we get into trouble, is when we listen to our heads or our minds, instead of our heart, or we try to rationalize why we feel a certain way, or try to talk ourselves out of it. This is a big mistake! You can end up causing many problems and troubles that again, are unnecessary. If the chela or individual would learn to listen to the heart and what the Master is trying to tell him through his heart, life would be so much simpler and we would all have the spiritual progress and awareness we desire.

Chapter Seven
April 13, 2008

Initiations and the Ego
Structure of Initiations

L ast night I was speaking about initiations. I got a little side-tracked, and only talked about one aspect of the initiations. Today I would like to continue with that subject. The order of the initiations and the way in which they are done, either on the outer or strictly on the inner, has been a cause for confusion for some people. Originally, we had a number of initiations and structured them so that people could have a greater understanding of the various levels of initiation, the responsibilities and abilities that come with these initiations, and generally how long it could or should take an individual to reach each of these initiations, or go from one level of initiation to the next.

Unfortunately, most people did not understand that this was our reasoning, and started looking at initiations as badges, accomplishments, and started to let the ego get in there. They started to think this meant that they were above everyone else, and could tell everyone how to think and what to do, and the people of lower initiation thought they should be looking to the higher initiates here on the outer for guidance and direction. This is not true, and I really want to stress this!

This is why we (and when I say we here, I mean the Order of Dhunami Masters) have made most of the initiations a special and secret event between the chela and the Master alone, and why, if the Master doesn't guide you and ask you to talk about that experience, then you shouldn't. If you do, you're going to have a bit of karma to deal with, and the Masters will have to give you some more tests before you can be trusted with some more information and some more vibrations.

Once these people that are higher initiates start to have this ego complex and start to try to give guidance to those new to or starting out in these teachings, they are not working from the higher worlds anymore! They place themselves in the lower worlds, even though they are still an initiate of the higher worlds. They do not lose any initiation or spiritual ground here, they have simply lowered their consciousness. We should not ever do that. The Living Dhunami Master of the Time is the only one who can guide any chela.

Now, those of you that are higher initiates you can talk with the other chelas, and share your experiences, share your own techniques or what has worked for you, but do not tell them what to do, do not put yourself in the role of teacher or guide, and this goes for those of you who are holding classes as well. This is exactly why we say holding classes instead of teaching classes. Darwin used to have the people coming to his class occasionally take over, and run the class themselves, and this was very good. I think this is a wonderful idea for many reasons: 1) there is no established 'teacher' of a class if we take turns in presenting the class and operating the class, 2) it gives people experience for running their own classes, and starting their own, and 3) it brings people out of their shells, makes them less shy, like getting your feet wet a little at a time, easing into it.

Now, I am going to be very direct here, because this is important. I have stated here that I do not want higher initiates wearing initiations like badges or promotions – you're not exactly old war heroes. And I want to again clearly state, do not try to guide or act as a guide to any of the lower plane chelas, help them by relating your own experiences and by telling them to look to the Masters and the Inner Master.

Now, I also want to speak to the initiates new to this path, or those who haven't realized themselves as Soul yet – do not look at a person's level of initiation in these teachings. Someone who is at a lower step than yourself can sometimes help you more than someone working in the higher planes. I want each and every chela to be looking to the Living Dhunami Master of the Time or any one of the Masters in this Dhunami Order for guidance and direction, and no one else here on this physical plane. I stated this and wrote about it in the late 1960s and in 1970, and Darwin spoke about it again in the late 1970s and very early 80s, but people either got confused about what we were saying or were not listening.

For this reason, the initiations are to stay as they are in these teachings. This means, the chela studies for two years, and then is eligible for the Light and Sound Initiation, which is technically called the Second Initiation because the First happens on the inner planes between the Master and the chela. After two years of study, the chela can request the Light and Sound Initiation, but it is up to the Living Dhunami Master of the Time to determine whether or not this individual is ready for that next step. If he or she is, then the Light and Sound Initiation can be given by the Living Dhunami Master with the aid of any Designated Sound Worker/Initiator.

This is also something that needs to be clarified. The Living Dhunami Master of the Time always gives the initiation, and I mean always, regardless of if the initiation is on the inner or on the outer. The only reason we have these outer initiations, and Initiators, is because this 'Initiator' helps the chela to focus, and helps to raise his or her vibrations so that the initiation can take place, so that the Master can raise that chela into the next highest area. This is all. That's all the Initiator is doing, which when you think about it, is not too much. These Initiators are simply there to aid the Living Dhunami Master with his inner work – and that is all they are doing when they are helping with an initiation. I would like people to realize this, and when they say, 'so-and-so gave me the Light and Sound Initiation,' they are speaking incorrectly. They should be saying, 'this individual helped me to get the Light and Sound Initiation, which was given to me by the Living Dhunami Master.'

Now the Soul Initiation, which is the only other one to be done on the physical, the individual is eligible for three years from the time of the Light and Sound Initiation. I urge you to take your time, because three years is nothing compared to the time we have left and have spent as Human Beings. Darwin always stated that we need to build a strong spiritual foundation, and he's right. That is more important and should be to the chela than getting an initiation.

So the Soul Initiation can be had at least three years after the Light and Sound Initiation, but this one the chela does not request. This is up to the Designated Sound Worker and the Living Dhunami Master of the Time. They'll know when you're ready. Please, do not become perturbed or upset about this if you do not have a Designated Sound Worker, or one close by, because these initiates, who are placed in this role, are actually dealing with and helping the Master work with many chelas over a large area. No one is left out, I can assure you. The Soul Initiation works just like the Light and Sound Initiation, in that the chela will be notified if they are to receive it, and an Initiator will be present in the physical, helping the individual to realize and handle the new vibrations. As stated before, the Living Dhunami Master of the Time always gives the initiation.

The Soul Initiation is the last one to be done on the physical plane, with the help of an Initiator. All others are done on the inner strictly between the Master and the chela, and there is an initiation for every plane of the inner worlds, up to fourteen, as stated in the Shariyat-Ki-Sugmad Book II, last chapter. If anyone should need further clarification on the subject of initiations they should refer to that book, but I want everyone to be very clear on the structure of the initiations, and why they are done this way. This is up to the Sugmad and the Order of Dhunami Masters, and no one else. No one on this physical plane should suggest anything else, or present to the Living Dhunami Master to change the present arrangement, because it is just as it needs to be – just like everything else.

I want to carefully state here and make clear to everyone that any initiation given by myself or Darwin Gross can never be lost or taken away, nor can any future initiation by the new Living Dhunami Master be taken away or lost. This has actually been talked about to a good degree in the teachings already, in my earlier writings as well as Darwin's. When we state that no chela can really turn away from the path, or step off the path, this is what we mean by that. When Darwin wrote the book You Can't Turn Back, this is exactly what he was talking about, and is exactly what he wanted people to realize at the time that he wrote the book.

When I stated earlier that the chela can ignore the Master, but that is all, I meant nothing has changed spiritually for the individual who is not studying under the true Living Dhunami Master of the Time, no matter what else the chela is doing, has done, and no matter who else the chela has looked to for spiritual guidance. Once we establish ourselves on a spiritual plane, which is done in the initiation, we will be on that plane regardless of what happens in our lives until we take active steps towards the next plane of spiritual enlightenment. I want each and every one of you to know the Sugmad loves you, and would not take away that which you have earned for yourself. No one can take away your level of initiation, which you have earned through your own spiritual exercises.

Chapter Eight
April 14, 2008

Dhunami Saints
Importance of Balance

The Path of the Saints in these teachings has not been written about or talked about much at all. I mentioned it occasionally, or mentioned that someone was a Saint, like Shamus-i-Tabriz. I don't think Darwin talked about the Saints at all. I want to say that it is important for people to have an understanding of the general principles in Dhunami before trying to understand the Path of the Saints, because one can easily get confused.

When one thinks of a Saint in this physical world, the images of St. Teresa probably come to mind – she was a wonderful woman. The Dhunami Saints do not walk around this physical plane trying to save the world or save societies, or uplift societies. A Dhunami Saint is different from a Dhunami Master in these teachings, although technically they are the same, because Saints are Masters. The difference is that Dhunami Saints are primarily concerned with the inner worlds, and working there – directly with the Soul bodies. A Dhunami Master does help with the inner work, but is also concerned with the physical world, helping the Living Dhunami Master of the Time with his mission – gathering up the Souls who wish to reach God this lifetime.

So the Dhunami Masters help the Living Dhunami Master with his mission, both on the inner and on the outer, whereas the Dhunami Saints have specialized areas that they work in, with individual Souls, on the Inner Planes of existence. These areas can be working with sick children, working with animals, or any other specific area in which Souls need help on the inner planes. The Dhunami Saints work primarily in their Soul bodies. This is why, even though you may call on one, like Prajapati (the animal Master), he is there although you probably won't see him.

When a Soul develops him or herself to the higher planes, those above the Soul plane, that individual can begin to learn certain talents or abilities, or techniques in a specific area, like working with children, being a healer, or any other specialized area, or specific area of work. I want to say something here about the healing that one can learn to do in Dhunami. Most healers are using the psychic energies to help injured or sick people with pain and to try to dissolve or get rid of their affliction. The healer in Dhunami who has developed himself to the areas above the Soul plane, and is working and dwelling there, uses absolutely no psychic energies or techniques to heal. This individual allows Divine Spirit to work through him, and Divine Spirit does the healing, not the individual.

This is the same with any individual, who is working from the higher planes, especially those who have chosen the Path of the Dhunami Saints, because all they are doing basically is being a conscious open (and when I say open, I mean *really* open) vehicle for the Divine Spirit. The Divine Spirit does all the work. I am stating this clearly because I do not want people in these teachings or people in general to look to the Dhunami Saints of this path for anything – they can do nothing, it is the Divine Spirit working though them and with them that creates the miracles. So, I am telling you here, if you look to Divine Spirit, and to the Living Dhunami Master of the Time, that you will have all that you need. You will have everything Divine Spirit is able to give you based on your level of consciousness.

I want to clarify here, to make sure this is clear, when an individual is learning about working in a certain area, like healing or working with children, one is learning how to let the Divine Spirit work through him or herself to do this particular job. The individual learning about this special area does so in the higher worlds, and before reaching the twelfth plane the individual is given a choice, to continue to work with the Living Dhunami Master of the Time, or to go into the area of Sainthood, and work with Divine Spirit in a specialized area. Individuals are needed in both areas. Many women go into the area of Sainthood, but they do not have to if they prefer not to.

Many Masters who have chosen to work with the Living Dhunami Master of the Time and not travel the Path of the Saints can develop that area after they have translated from this physical plane. Almost all the Guardians of the Wisdom Temples are Saints, even though they were Masters who worked closely with the Living Dhunami Master of the Time here on earth. So, on this path one should never feel as though anything is kept from him, or that he cannot do certain things. All things are possible in Divine Spirit.

As long as we keep ourselves balanced and our attention on Divine Spirit, then we are able to make progress in our spiritual goals, and we can realize or understand anything. But the key is to stay in balance, and this is more complicated than it sounds at first.

Every time the chela gets 'out of balance,' the Living Dhunami Master of the Time or the Masters of the Dhunami Order have to work to get that chela back into balance. This is why it is stated the chela should always walk the middle path, which is also called the Narrow Way. Now, there are two ways the chela can get out of balance, one is in the mental area, and the other is in the emotional area. Many people have problems understanding this, and so we're going to try to clarify some of it.

When we get too far off to the left is when we are in the emotional world. Now balance is a tricky sort of thing, very delicate, because we do not want to be like robots out here, and we do not have any problems or issues with people feeling emotions. If you want to cry, or to be angry or upset or you are feeling that way, go with it, let it flow, but when that has passed, or that moment that has caused you to feel that way has passed, let it go. Then you should do something to make yourself feel better, or have a spiritual exercise because everything on this physical plane must be a balance.

Most of this has to do with living in the moment, because if we are in the moment, we are not thinking about and worrying about what we have to do tomorrow, which can get us out of balance on the mental side. If we're living in the moment we're not upset about that person that may have said something not so nice about us, getting us out of balance on the emotional side. Again, I'm not saying here that we have to neglect our duties, or that we shouldn't plan for tomorrow, what I am saying here is that we should not be dwelling on it, or staying in that state of consciousness.

If one finds it difficult to live in the moment, which most of you will when you start to try to do it, use the Divine Spirit. Place your attention on the Master, or any of the Masters, or the Light or Sound, and keep putting your attention back to that. You will soon find that you cannot seem to hold your attention on much else. Some of you are probably beginning to recognize that the techniques discussed in these teachings for the spiritual and contemplative exercises are also techniques used when we are walking around in our daily lives. It has also been stated that one could do a spiritual or contemplative exercise while walking down the street or any other place that one should find himself, if he hasn't the time to sit down and do it.

The reason I am telling you to walk around chanting or singing the spiritual words, which I spoke about earlier, as well as keeping your attention on the Master, or Divine Spirit, or Divine Love, is because if we are dwelling or living in a contemplative state almost all of the time, then we are really being clear open vehicles for Sugmad and the Masters.

I want people to take their time with this. It certainly is helpful in one's spiritual growth and progress, but it is not necessary. All that is necessary is the twenty to thirty minute spiritual or contemplative exercise in a twenty-four hour period. Especially for the new person, or those in their first few years in these teachings, this is what I really want you to focus on. This is building the spiritual foundation that Darwin was talking about. Because when I say there is only one spiritual or contemplative exercise needed in a twenty-four hour period, I mean it when I say it is needed. I cannot stress enough the importance of these spiritual exercises and contemplative exercises, especially for the new person.

Now, I want to say here, if you are struggling with this, or forget, or miss having it for a little while, don't beat yourself up. Because there is always this moment, or the next to have a spiritual or contemplative exercise, and if one desires to have discipline concerning these exercises, it will be developed within that individual with Divine Spirit. When you realize that Divine Spirit takes care of the littlest things in this world, like how the individual cells in your bodies work together, to the biggest things, like running the universes, and making sure planets stay in orbit and don't smack into each other, then you suddenly realize that everything is taken care of, and that what you do from day to day is not that big of a deal. If you forget to or just don't do your spiritual or contemplative exercises, the world has not ended, things go on just as they do, and you should too.

I want to say that there are many things the chela has to work out when he or she first steps on this path of Dhunami, but if we have an open mind, Spirit will work with us and through us, and many things can and will be worked out or corrected without the chela having to know anything about it. It does not matter if the chela takes fifteen, fifty, or five hundred years in getting to the Soul plane, and having Self-realization. What matters is that he or she is trying.

Chapter Nine
April 15, 2008

Finding, Discovering, and Experiencing Truth
Uncovering Divine Love

M an gets caught up in his daily activities, his daily responsibilities, and he soon forgets all about God and Divine Spirit. I have said many things so far in this book, which could also be found in many of my other books, but what I have not talked much about yet is Truth. The only real Truth can be found at the Temple Within, when we do our spiritual or contemplative exercises, when we are in direct contact with the Light and Sound and the Masters. I do not want people to confuse Light with Truth, because Light is wisdom, or knowledge. This knowledge from the Light is what helps to raise our level of consciousness and our level of awareness. The Divine Love will touch us, and flood us, if we allow it to. With this Divine Love comes Truth, about ourselves, and about the Sugmad or God. Without an understanding of this Truth it is impossible to reach the God-consciousness state.

This Truth that I am speaking of has to do with the paradoxes I mentioned before, most of which can be found in <u>Stranger by the River</u>. Now the Truth is unable to be realized unless we have a great deal of love within us. If an individual makes a study of <u>Stranger by</u>

the River, which is the idea with the present discourse, one would realize there are only a few simple concepts here, which include love, truth, surrender, and the mind and ego. There are some others, but these are the main ones. The Divine Love is the most important one of all these and really, if one put their attention on this and really worked on having love within himself, almost all other negativities would drop away. And so that is basically what we are trying to do with the spiritual and contemplative exercises here, is to get the individual to recognize and realize Divine Love.

Sometimes it is easier to understand something by recognizing everything it isn't. This is the idea that if we eliminate certain concepts or ideas, we can better understand something. Now people think the opposite of love, or the negation or absence of love is hatred, but that is only one aspect. There are several, but the one I want to talk about right now is fear. When we have fear, or feel fear, it is a lack of love within us, as well as a lack of trust in the Masters and Divine Spirit. Fear is a negative aspect of this world that is often used to control people, or to influence their behavior, but if you are filled with Divine Love then the fear cannot get to you.

I would like to tell you all that there is absolutely nothing in this world to be afraid of, nor in the inner worlds. People cause fear within themselves when they worry that they are going to make a mistake, or aren't going to make the right choice. This is also called worry, anxiety, and restlessness, but it really is just fear. Divine Spirit, the Masters, and the Sugmad love each individual more than they can understand. There is no reason for us to ever cause fear within ourselves, and we should not let others put fear in us, because as I said before, this blocks out the love.

I want each and every Soul to remember that this is a training ground, and I mean that literally. We are here to learn, and many of us will need to stumble a little bit, or get off in the wrong direction a little, perhaps make what man refers to as mistakes, and we should be happy for and grateful for these experiences because only through these experiences are we going to realize ourselves and reach Soul and God-realization here and now. The Masters do not blame anyone, and we do not judge anyone, that is not for us to do. The Lords of Karma are required to keep a balance in this world, but the Masters will help the chela to work off that karma, swifter than the mind can grasp. If you happen to stumble a bit along this path, we will be there helping you up, and we'll try to help you have a sense of humor about it, so that you can laugh about it, because it is not a negative thing, this learning process.

Some of us will have less stumbles on this path, or less excursions, but that is because they went through it in a previous lifetime. Each chela earns where they are, and they in a sense earn the opportunity to stumble, so as I said before, this is not something to worry about, or be ashamed about, or be afraid of, because we are all here to learn. None of us got it right the first time. Well, I should say hardly any, because perhaps there were one or two. My point here is that there are no mistakes as man thinks of mistakes, there are no wrong moves, because each step we take, even if it is away from the God-man, the Living Dhunami Master of the Time, it really is toward the Sugmad because through that experience, through those steps, we will learn how and what we are doing and what we are trying to accomplish here.

I hope that each one of you can understand that every stumble we make, every step we take away from the Sugmad is one more step leading us back. It is only through these steps that we can uncover ourselves, the love within ourselves, and eventually reach God-realization. Know that even though you may stumble, and even though you may fall, the Masters have Divine Love for you, and will be there to guide you. The Sugmad has great love for you, or you would not be here, with the opportunity to work with IT and dwell in ITs home.

I would like to touch tonight a little on the subject of insecurity. Insecurity is when we feel like we're not good enough, or the work we do is inadequate, or we can't seem to get much right. This is a complex within the individual that seems to stem from a low self-esteem, as man calls it. The spiritual reasons for this complex include: not trusting the Master, not accepting or realizing our own Divinity, and a lack of love for ourselves.

This is an issue many Souls are dealing with and I know there are many methods man has tried to use to correct this complex. I don't know of any that have been very successful. Psychiatry is a useful science, in that it teaches man a lot about his own mind, and helps him to discover the cause or causes for many of his behaviors. But until man realizes that the mind cannot solve the problems it has created, or cannot solve its own problems, he will continue to suffer from them, having only marginal relief.

Now, some people do have chemical imbalances, so to speak, and some people really do need psychiatric care. I am not telling anyone to stay away from psychiatry or counseling, all I am saying here is that if one would apply him or herself to the spiritual exercises, one could have much greater results, and save himself time and money. The mind is a tool only, but when it is able to rule the body, and itself, instead of Soul running the show, we will have a difficult time of seeing our way clear of problems. The mind loves to have something to chew over, which in turn usually causes anxiety and worry, and can have physical effects on the individual. This is how powerful the mind is. It is a very useful tool, and really man is only using a small portion of what could be used. But the mind is so powerful, and if we let it run amok, or do what it wants, we would be a mess. It is like a small child in that it needs discipline and guidance.

There are many ways to achieve this, but the most effective I know of are the spiritual and contemplative exercises of Dhunami. Instead of the mind ruling the body, it should be Soul, because Soul can have and experience Divine Love, which purifies the man in every sense of the word, and helps to improve his life. Whenever an individual would ask me, what they can do to help themselves, I would tell them to practice the spiritual exercises or contemplative exercises, and if they'd like to contemplate on something, to contemplate on Divine Love. One could do this for years, and still desire to do it more, because when you get even just one drop of this Divine Love, you want buckets more, and you wonder at how to get it. Divine Spirit is a giving substance, in that It comes into contact with us to uplift us, to purify us and to help us to reach Self and God-realization.

Man first recognizes this love in woman, either in the mother, the sister, girlfriend, wife, or just a friend sometimes, but women have more love in them to begin with than men, generally. By recognizing this love in women, and when women recognize it in themselves, this creates a desire in them for more of it, and to have it within themselves. And so it has been said that woman is the greatest vehicle the Sugmad has for love, and this is why women are the life-givers of this human race. Some people recognize this love right away in their mother. Some people recognize a lack of it in their own mother when they come into contact with other women, and some people do not recognize this love until they reach adulthood, but everyone does eventually.

So this awakens the search in man for love, what he thinks of as love, which is really a form of Divine Love, and he'll continue searching until he thinks he has found it, and will stand proud and happy, until he realizes later that what he has found, hasn't fulfilled him the way he thought it would, and then he'll continue searching. Sometimes it can take lifetimes, but man finally ends his search for Divine Love when he finds the Godman, the Living Dhunami Master of the Time, and then his journey has begun.

Chapter Ten
April 16, 2008

Surrender and Individuality

Today I want to talk about surrender. Many people do not understand this subject of surrender, as it is very paradoxical. To surrender while still retaining our individuality is key to spiritual growth, and like anything else, if the chela desires to surrender, an understanding of the subject will be given through Divine Spirit and the Masters.

Anytime we give a class, give out a book, talk with someone about the teachings, or leave a brochure, we are doing Divine Spirit's will or Sugmad's will. Some people mistake this for having surrendered, and to an extent it is, but not in the capacity that is necessary, and not as the Masters would like. Doing all or any of the aforementioned things means the individual is fulfilling their responsibility to Divine Spirit, the Sugmad and the Masters and it means this person is or will be working off karma and helping themselves to unfold.

However, when we have really surrendered, we are receiving instruction from Divine Spirit and the Masters in our spiritual and contemplative exercises, and we are actively using this instruction in our spiritual matters and in our daily lives. This instruction can and often does range from something as simple as where to get your haircut, to where to leave that Dhunami book so the right person will find it, or the person who is ready to pick up the teachings. It will also let us know where and when to hold a class, where we should move, if at all, and instruction in our spiritual lives as to how to open ourselves more and unfold our own consciousness.

I cannot think of a single matter the Divine Spirit will not advise you on, as long as you ask, and are receptive and able to hear the answer. It does not matter if you are a Master of your own universe, if you are an 8th initiate, or a 2nd initiate, if you are not doing your spiritual exercises then you will not be attuned to that guidance and instruction.

Now the surrender comes in when the chela learns that Spirit can and will care for every aspect of our lives, if we allow it into our space, and allow it to work through us. The individual can begin by stating to themselves everyday 'thy will be done, of myself I can do nothing, I surrender.' Any one of these will get the point across to Divine Spirit and the Masters that you want to surrender. Now, I cannot stress enough the importance of doing the spiritual exercises while trying to surrender. Often, the chela asks for surrender, but doesn't really understand the concept of surrender, or what it means to surrender. I know of many chelas who have learned the hard way – this is when a chela asks for guidance and asks to surrender, but does not give up haggling over the little things in the mind, or neglects the spiritual and contemplative exercises, or refuses to listen and apply advice or direction when it is given.

This individual makes life harder on him or herself than it needs to be, because when this happens everything seems to go wrong. When we start to struggle against the Divine Spirit and the Masters, it can only muddle things up, because Divine Spirit can see and knows everything. And we, from our limited mindset sometimes will try to say to ourselves 'well maybe IT's not quite right about that,' or, 'I don't quite believe that,' or, 'I think I'm going to do it this way.' All of a sudden the individual realizes he is having a hard time of things, which are progressively getting harder, and then to top it all off we stub our toe or smack our heads, and we throw our hands up and say, 'that's it, I give up,' or, 'I quit, I don't want to play anymore.' And these little statements of themselves, because they are tied with such feeling, are the act of surrendering.

Now, why do we continue to struggle against Divine Spirit when we have already decided we want to surrender? Because usually the individual doesn't really understand the concept of surrender when he or she asks for it, and because if we surrender ourselves to Divine Spirit and the Masters, then the mind and the ego are no longer in control, and they hate that. They don't want to give up; they like being in control, so this is where the struggle comes in. If we are careful, we can avoid this by having the feeling attached to the saying in our daily statement of surrender, but this is difficult to do, to conjure up an emotion on demand that we are unfamiliar with.

Another way to avoid the struggle is to try and recognize when our minds and our egos start to get in there, and start to pick apart the instruction and the guidance and direction. If we recognize this right away we can stop it. We can make the conscious choice of who we are going to listen to: our egos, or 'little selves,' or Divine Spirit and the Masters. It is difficult to recognize which is which at first but a good rule of thumb is to ask yourself 'what is my motivation or the reasoning for this action?' If it is selfish you can bet it is the ego every time. If instead you can say, 'this motivation or reasoning is for the benefit of all individuals involved including myself,' then it is pretty safe to say that it is Divine Spirit directing us. It takes time to develop this discerning capability within ourselves, so be patient with it as with any unfoldment technique you are trying. We have all the time in the world and even much more than that.

Sometimes we have to go through these lessons only once, sometimes it is twice, and sometimes it is 5 times. Some people learn surrender, they go through the struggle, they begin to understand, and they finally throw their hands up with feeling and truly surrender, and they do fine with it for a while, and then they start to lose track of the ego a bit and it starts to try to gain control again and do its own will, satisfy its own wants. And we don't always recognize this and so sometimes we get more stubbed toes, or more smacks on the head, but only if we truly desire them. There is no shame in needing or experiencing more stubbed toes because these spiritual lessons we are trying to learn here are tricky, because when we say them or talk about them they sound so simple. It is applying them, understanding them deeply, and living them that is the tough part. And it matters not how many times we have a bump or a smack, what matters is that we will eventually learn.

I remember an old comic I saw once, that had two men talking and a third man walks by with a flat head, and says hello to one of the men. The other man asks why the passerby's head was flat, and the one who knew him replied 'he's hit his head on the hood of his car so many times while trying to fix it, it's gone flat.' And the other man said, 'he must be a helluva mechanic by now!' Take your time, go slow, do your spiritual and contemplative exercises, and have Divine Love. That is all one needs to know.

Some of you are probably wondering about the individuality part. People used to ask me all the time if they are surrendering and they are doing the will of Divine Spirit and Sugmad, how are they still an individual? Here's the thing – each person has free will and if you are deciding to allow Divine Spirit to work through you, that is making an individual decision. You can choose to ignore the Masters and Divine Spirit, which is another example of exercising your individuality and free will.

In these teachings by gaining Self and God-realization we are able to retain our individuality for eternity, and become conscious co-workers with Divine Spirit and the Sugmad. When I say individuality or individual, I am referring to Soul Itself. If the person is able to reach the Soul plane and have Self-realization, they are going to have conscious awareness of their existence, their actions, and their work throughout eternity. If the individual does not want this, they can choose to become one with the Sugmad, to become a particle in ITs atomic structure, and that is fine, but I prefer to keep my consciousness, my awareness, and my individuality. I know this is difficult to understand but if you contemplate on it, this will become clear to you.

This has been stated before, that the inner life is the true existence, and this life is a training ground which allows us to develop our consciousness so that we can be conscious of our inner lives. This is why it takes time for the person to have experiences in these teachings, because it takes an awakening or an opening of the consciousness and the awareness for the individual to remember an experience. This is in a sense waking up. While we are asleep, we cannot see and have experiences on this physical plane and so it is with the inner worlds, the true spiritual worlds. While we are here on this physical plane, it takes a little waking up of the consciousness to allow us to have experiences in the spiritual worlds.

Retaining your individuality is a choice, as stated before. Every step on this path is a choice. The Masters, and the Living Dhunami Master of the Time will never push you or rush you, and every step of the way is your decision. When I heard I could retain my individuality, I was skeptical. When I started to understand that my spiritual experiences were real, and in fact more real than this physical life or world, I was ecstatic! Of course, it has to be a balance in all things but it is alright to get excited or be happy about it. Our individuality, our consciousness, is all that we really have, and it is all that we can take with us when we translate. I'd like to think that people will begin to understand this in time, but the masses are not necessarily very eager or ready for this kind of information. It takes a very unique Being to read what is written here and think, 'boy, I like the sound of that,' or, 'I'd like to try these teachings, because what this man is saying here is intriguing.' I have always said that Divine Spirit chooses us, not the other way around. Some people don't like this, because they think it means they don't have free will or that I am trying to communicate some sort of destiny, but neither of those are the case. I am simply saying here that Divine Spirit sees those of us who are ready for this kind of information, or may be receptive to the Masters, and it helps those people to come across a book, or a brochure, or a person who is spilling Divine Love and radiates Divine Spirit.

Chapter Eleven
April 17, 2008

Divine Spirit
Function of the Living Dhunami Master

N ow I want to discuss the subject of Divine Spirit. I have used this term often in this book, and DapRen used it very often. Many of you already have an idea of what Divine Spirit is, but for some of you who are not sure or are not so clear, I'd like to make an explanation here. Divine Spirit is the pure substance from the Sugmad that flows out of the Sugmad down to all the planes, including the physical. IT is the essence of God, not ITs breath, but ITs essence. IT carries the Divine Love with IT, and when IT flows through those who are open to IT, and have developed themselves enough to be vehicles for IT, those individuals feel the Divine Love, and IT reaches other people through them, as well as lifts them up.

Now the Divine Spirit cannot be as potent, so to speak, here as it is in the higher planes, because of the negativity here, because of the vibrations here, and because of our bodies and states of consciousness. The more developed we are as far as consciousness, the more Divine Spirit and Divine Love we are able to handle. This Divine Spirit is the essence of life. Divine Spirit is that which purifies us, IT is that which uplifts us and raises our vibrations. IT is that which heals us, IT is that which brings us happiness and joy – which is why Darwin always used to say the distinguishing factor or characteristic of those following this path is an innate joy and cheerfulness. Divine Spirit is also that which gives us those bumps on the head sometimes, those difficulties and trials we need to open ourselves up to IT more, to be a vehicle for more of IT. If IT can accomplish this without many bumps to the head, or shins IT will do so, but some of us are stubborn. I know I was.

Now don't misunderstand me here – I'm not saying that some invisible force is going to be hitting you over the head. Of course, Divine Spirit isn't exactly invisible, it can be seen as Light and heard as Sound, but my point here is that there are no coincidences, and if we are talking or thinking negatively about an individual and suddenly we run into the coffee table, we should be aware that this is Divine Spirit letting us know we are reacting or acting negatively, and to stop. Again, this will only happen if we are open to IT, and are asking for help with our spiritual growth.

Now some individuals say that if Divine Spirit does all of this, why do we need the Godman, the Living Dhunami Master of the Time? Many reasons: One, or I should say the first is, we need him to set our feet upon the path, to bring us into the Divine Spirit, the current, and when we are initiated by him, this is what he is doing, he is lifting us into the current of Divine Spirit at a higher vibration rate than we are currently. So we need him for the initiations, we need him to also help us learn our lessons. If all we had was the Divine Spirit bumping us on the head every time we did something counter-productive to our spiritual progress, well frankly some of us would be getting bumped constantly. The Living Dhunami Master of the Time works with us to get rid of these negative habits and actions that cause karmic conditions and keep us from realizing ourselves as Soul, our true identity. He helps us to avoid these bumps, so that maybe we get one or two at most, instead of fifty. He introduces us slowly to the flow of Divine Spirit, so we don't get out of balance. He gives us the spiritual protection in this world as well as the other planes. He teaches us to be open and receptive to the Divine Spirit so it can flow through us, as it flows through him.

And really the list goes on and on. There are so many reasons to allow the Living Dhunami Master of the Time to guide us, that it would take a whole book just to list them all. The most important, in my opinion, and the one that was most important to me when I was first coming onto this path, is that the Living Dhunami Master of the Time is a Spiritual Traveler. He has traveled the lower worlds, and the higher worlds, knows the Beings in charge or rulers of each plane, and knows what needs to be learned or accomplished in order to rise above or travel beyond these planes. Without the Living Dhunami Master of the Time, the individual could spend many lifetimes on a single plane, such as the astral or causal plane, and many individuals do. When we become a student of the Living Dhunami Master of the Time, all we are really doing is allowing him to guide us through the lower worlds as quickly and as smoothly as possible, and plant our feet and awareness on the Soul plane. And even after that, he will continue to guide us with the help of other Masters of the Dhunami Order. He is a guide, a way-shower, and only he can swiftly take an individual to the higher states of consciousness.

Chapter Twelve
April 18, 2008

Exploring the Worlds Beyond
Divine Spirit and Our Vibrations
Trusting Our Experiences

I always wondered what the other worlds were like, meaning the inner planes, the spiritual planes of existence. When I found a way to explore them, I latched onto it like a leech and I didn't want to let go. I wanted more and more, faster and faster, and I had to have bumps on the head as well, as I was speaking of the other night. You can never go too slow in these teachings, but you can certainly go too fast. I stated before it is very important to go slow and have a spiritual foundation built up. I got rather unbalanced for a time, and had to take a look at myself and what I was doing. Sometimes that is the best thing we can do for ourselves, is to step away and take a look at ourselves, where we are working from whether it is emotional or mental, and take the time to get ourselves back into balance.

When I first had the Light in my spiritual and contemplative exercises, I thought that was it. I thought that was God and that I had reached Heaven, but then, a while later, when I got a little of the Sound, I thought that was it, but then I got a little more, some shapes and some higher vibration Sounds. Many people have experiences on the astral plane, which looks very much like this plane only brighter, bigger, and a little better vibrationally, and people think this is heaven. It is okay to think that what you've got or what you're experiencing is the best, but you should keep asking for more. I always wanted more, more of what I already had, which I thought was the best. Through this yearning, this desire within myself, I was able to unfold myself to the next highest region every time.

I never knew what the next plane was going to be like, I wasn't even sure there was one, but I was determined to find out. It takes hard work – having the discipline, focus, and ability to sit still and do the spiritual exercises. So I am saying here that if you are having an experience, that is wonderful, but to keep looking, keep going, because the higher you go, the finer the vibrations get, and the subtler things get, and the brighter things get. If one wishes to make a study of it all, he or she can do so within himself, at the Temple Within with the Living Dhunami Master of the Time or another Dhunami Master. It takes time to develop oneself to a greater area, but over time one can learn everything one desires or wishes to learn about these other planes of existence.

A study can also be made of The Tiger's Fang, the original version, as it has changed a little over the years, but this book chronicles my experiences in the other worlds, and in great detail explains what they are like, as well as some pitfalls the individual could fall into on that particular plane. I want each person who steps on this path to reach whatever goals they have set for themselves, no matter how big or small, and all the Masters of this Dhunami Order will work with you so that you can realize these goals, no matter how long it takes.

The astral plane is very vivid, very colorful, with many vehicles, buildings – it is similar to the physical plane. There is a museum here that one can visit if one wishes that shows many inventions that have not been brought to Earth yet. One can visit this museum if he or she so desires, but do not get caught up here, because there are many other things to see and experience in these spiritual planes. The following planes get less and less cluttered, less busy, finer in Sound, Light and vibrations, until we reach the area where there is no form, no shapes as man thinks of it. This has confused some people, that since they are seeing less things they think they are missing something, or that their spiritual eye has stopped working.

I am encouraging all of you to go on your feelings a bit more, how do you feel when you see this Light, when you hear this Sound, and you'll find the more subtle it gets, the more Divine Love you will feel. It needs to be progressively less and less like that, so as not to be a shock to the consciousness, but I know once you realize where you are, what is happening, and you feel the Divine Love coming through, you will be ecstatic as I was, and still am. That feeling that we get in our spiritual and contemplative exercises can stay with us the whole day, and It wants to. It doesn't want to get shut out or shut off when we're done with our twenty minutes, or thirty, or whatever it is we do on a daily basis. Learn to develop that, to carry it with you, for it is much simpler than man can understand at first, how to carry it with us through the day. Darwin spoke of this, and if one contemplates on it, it will be told to him or her. There is no reason, except when we are holding ourselves back, to feel a lack of Divine Love.

I know that many of you have been searching for some time for something to fulfill yourselves, for something to fill a perceived void in yourself. The first thing I would like to say is that there is no such void, only our own lack of recognition of that which is within us. Secondly, do not take my word for what is written here, do the spiritual exercises outlined, chant HU, and you will know the answer, because it will be shown to you, and it will be your answer, not given to you by anyone else, developed by the mind or based on emotions, but it will be a true experience.

Now I want each individual to make up their own minds and their own decisions. Too often chelas or students on this path listen to what other people are saying – in other words, they take the answer they got at the Temple Within with the Master, and they start to question it, and they drag it down into the mental world and try to dissect it, and find some facts of logical reasoning for their answers. What saddens me the most is that sometimes it is another Dhunami chela that tries to get an individual or another chela to examine their experiences. First of all, if you are having experiences with the Master or Divine Spirit at the Temple Within, you should feel very blessed, loved, and grateful, and you should not be second-guessing that experience, or trying to validate it in some manner.

Now usually a person who has just started to have these experiences will wonder, and will doubt them, but soon after the chela discovers through some other situation that what the Masters or Divine Spirit told him on the inner was correct and true. Sometimes this is enough of an explanation for the chela, but for other people they still go on wondering 'was that real,' or, 'was the Master or Divine Spirit right about that?' Soon, through all this doubting, questioning and lowering of vibrations, the person finds that Divine Spirit and the Masters aren't telling them anything anymore. Not because the Masters have given up on this individual, but because the individual has given up on the Masters and Divine Spirit, and no longer has much faith or belief.

When doubts are alive in a person's consciousness, and they feel like something is not going to happen, then it won't. This is what I mean when I say we must be receptive to Divine Spirit and the Order of Dhunami Masters, and open. Also, for that individual who is encouraging people to question their experiences with Divine Spirit and the Masters, there is karma attached with that, because we can only relate our own experiences and knowledge – we should never tell anyone what to do, this is getting in their space, invading their space, unless of course they ask for our advice. The Masters and Divine Spirit will give you time. Don't feel like you have to know right away. We don't expect blind faith, and we don't want it, we want you to question us, but not forever. We need faith and belief in these teachings just like any other if we are to get anywhere.

Many times a student will ask why a certain situation happened, or why something is the way it is, and all these answers can be found within yourself, should you have the desire, the openness, and the patience to find them for yourself. It baffles me sometimes how people feel they need to go find God, so they go to the mountains, or they go to churches, or they go to meditation classes, or they go into austerities, and none of this is necessary. The only way to find God is by looking within ourselves.

As babies we first discover emotion, and then as toddlers we find our minds, and spend most of our lives trying to develop our minds, when what we really need to do is go back to being children, before our minds began to take over, get back in touch with that emotion, that innocence and love, for that is the only way to find God, for God is the simplest of all things, and that is why it is so difficult to understand. Some people wonder why it takes so long, and it is because we need to completely throw out everything that the mind knows, and get rid of the mind before we can begin to get a glimpse of God.

Chapter Thirteen
April 19, 2008

Releasing Tension
Relaxation Technique

Today I would like to begin with a subject that affects many people, whether or not they realize it. I am talking about stress, anxiety, tension, that which keeps our bodies in a tense state and our minds wrapped up in the mental world. Many individuals do not understand when they are being uptight, or when they are tense. We have gotten in the habit of neglecting our bodies, and not paying attention to them, but if we paid more attention to our bodies, we could recognize when our muscles are tensed up, when our palms are sweaty, and when our hearts are beating quickly. All of this is our bodies trying to tell us that we are tense.

The important thing to remember is that when our bodies are tense, or in an excited state, then the Divine Spirit or the Masters cannot reach us, and cannot help lift us into the higher planes. This tense state or excited state can be a trap, especially for those who are excited, and bouncing and happy, because everything must be a balance. There was a young man at one of my classes once, and he had an experience there, and he got very excited about it, and let his body get into an excited state, and he just had a hard time containing himself. I had to let him know after class that even though he was happy, and he had had a positive experience, that we as Spiritual Beings need to try to stay in balance – otherwise, we can block and stop that flow down to a trickle.

This is often a cause for frustration in the individual when one begins or tries to do a spiritual or contemplative exercise. We will have much more success with this if we can take a few moments and calm ourselves first, before trying to see anything or hear anything, or get an answer. One technique is to chant a higher powered word, such as Sugmad, or one from the higher planes, such as Huk or Aluk. These words carry with them such vibrations, that they are able to quickly clear the body of tension, stress, and negative emotion. And so if the individual would do this a few times, or for a few minutes before beginning the spiritual or contemplative exercise, he or she would have much more success, and be able to sit still for longer.

Now, if the individual continues to chant these higher words, this can be a little too much energy for the individual, and for the purpose of getting our answers and getting the awareness and vibrations slowly and gradually, your own word or HU should be used during the exercise. Again, one needs to go slow with this, and give it a few tries.

Another technique one can use is to wait to chant, and instead, for the first few moments just picture one of the Masters, or a place you would like to visit in the spiritual planes, and just breathe deeply as you visualize one of the Masters, or you can visualize a few, but one at a time.

These techniques can be used before bed as well, to relax the individual and allow him or her to drift off to sleep easier. Many people seem to have a problem with getting enough sleep these days, or falling asleep. Some of that comes from a lack of exercise, or too many sugars or stimulating foods before bed, but I think the majority of it comes from not being able to quiet down, quiet the mind and body. Sleep is more important than most people realize for a couple of reasons. Depriving the body and mind of sleep causes all sorts of problems internally. It is hard on the eyes, the immune system, the reflexes, and reasoning and logic abilities.

More importantly, however, is that sleep and dreams are a very important part of our spiritual development, in that we work things out in the dream state consciously or unconsciously, as far as karma and other situations. We are also visiting the Wisdom Temples at night, whether we are aware of it or not, and we are learning and unfolding. Also, the dreams that we are aware of can be very valuable in determining where we are spiritually, as well as what we are or should be working on. In addition, sometimes the answers we have requested, or the questions we have asked will be made clear in the dream state.

So it is important and very beneficial to ourselves to use these techniques and calm ourselves, whether it is before bed, before a contemplation, or any other part of the day where we feel we are tense and anxious. This can be done as often as needed, and whenever or wherever the individual may be. I have used this technique myself in my car, or in a bathroom before giving a lecture. If we are in a meeting, or at a lunch, we can excuse ourselves for a few moments and do this at our desk, or outside, getting some fresh air so to speak. This also keeps the individual from developing long term effects from tension and anxiety, things like ulcers and headaches, and other afflictions of the body.

Now, by using these techniques, all we are doing is relaxing the mind, even the subconscious mind. Many individuals say or think they are not tense, or stressed individuals because they do not constantly haggle over things, or worry over things, but just because we are not constantly thinking about something, this does not mean we are free of it, or that it does not bother us, or isn't affecting us. So by using the techniques I have discussed here, one is able to rise above these lower planes, and drop all of the negativity that is causing the tension in the mind and body. Without relaxing ourselves Divine Spirit is not able to reach us, because we have to quiet ourselves, and make ourselves able to receive the Divine Spirit, and Divine Love.

Once we have the Divine Love in our lives, and we latch onto it and keep ourselves open so that it will continue to flow through us, we find that every aspect of our lives has improved, and every negative aspect such as hate, fear, and tension and stress drop away. But again it is a process, and it takes time. You'll find the more you use these techniques of relaxation, that over time you hardly need to use them anymore.

I used to keep a journal where I would write down every technique or spiritual exercise for contemplation that I used, and I would keep track of it, and if after two weeks or a month it wasn't working for me, then I would move on to something else. But if it did work for me, then I would put a star by it, so that I would remember that it worked, and I could go back to it and use it if I needed to. And you'll notice the more you travel this path, and the more experiences you have, you'll get or come up with some of your own spiritual or contemplative exercises, and you'll see that these are the ones that work the best. But it all has to start somewhere, and I think relaxing oneself enough to have a spiritual or contemplative exercise is a great place to begin.

Chapter Fourteen
April 20, 2008

Continuity of the Living Dhunami Master
Choosing an Area of Service
Freedom in Dhunami

When a Master leaves this physical plane of existence, it should be a happy time and occasion for all those who knew him, all of his chelas, and all those who recognize him as a Spiritual Being. I can say for myself it was a happy time, and whenever a Spiritual Master translates from this physical plane, and finally drops the physical body for the last time after so many incarnations, so much struggle, and so much work, we have a great party or celebration on these inner planes. I want to tell you that because of the immense work the Masters do while they are on this physical plane, it really is such a joy to be free of the body, as it should be with all people.

When a Master initiates a chela onto this path, and into the Light and Sound, they make a promise or a pact with that person that the Master will guide the chela through the lower worlds, place them securely on the Soul plane, and will continue to work with the individual towards greater unfoldment should the chela desire.

Now, this does not change when the Master translates, he is still that chela's guide, and he is still responsible for that chela's spiritual growth. The work continues, even though he no longer has a physical body and is not initiating any more chelas. Rebazar Tarzs was still working with individuals he had initiated when he was the Living Dhunami Master of the Time when I was present on the physical plane, and probably still is to this day. I am still working with every chela I initiated who still desires help to unfold their awareness and reach greater spiritual heights. So nothing slows down for the Master when he finishes his work as the Living Dhunami Master. Many Masters will drop the physical body at this point, while a few will take on duties that require him to keep his body to serve on this planet or another. He does not retire as some individuals have stated or joked. In fact, he usually takes on more work, just of a different nature.

Many of the Masters who are working on the inner planes or on this physical plane have become guardians, such as Fubbi Quantz, Rami Nuri, and Lai Tsi. So this is just a continuation of work and service, but in a different area than they were working before. I am still the Mahanta, and will be for a number of years to come, a few hundred years. DapRen, who was my successor, is working with the Nine Silent Ones, those great Beings who serve the Sugmad directly.

So, what I am saying here is that just because a Master has translated or left this physical plane, does not mean he has stopped working with us or working for our unfoldment. Many people have said that they feel DapRen's presence even stronger now that he is free of his physical form. This is because he is able to move around better and at his own volition, more so than when he had a body to care for. It was the same for me and my chelas when I translated.

I want each person who steps on this path to know and understand that you have many Masters working with you, whether you are aware of it or not. Each Master has his or her place in the universe, and in the teachings, and thus in the development of certain areas within an individual. Many of these Masters we come into contact with in the Wisdom Temples, and they help with our wisdom and knowledge, teach us about the path, and help us with specific issues associated with whatever plane that Wisdom Temple is situated on.

It should be remembered that when one enters into the higher planes in these teachings and past the Self-realization area, we are developing ourselves to become of service: we are going to be in service to the Sugmad, the Masters, and these people who are searching for spiritual unfoldment. Those of us who have developed that factor of gratitude within ourselves, for the Masters and the Sugmad, will have an easier time of entering the higher spiritual planes and of being of service and helping with the work.

Now, as stated before, you can choose the area which you want to work with and there is just about everything you can imagine. Anything that interests you, or that you are passionate about, you can learn about, and work with. I am not saying it will all be easy, or that you will start right into that area with which you want to work or spend most of your time, because we as individuals must be purified for the work and prepared for the work.

I always smiled at those people who told me they were going to go to heaven after they die and just sit there, and just enjoy themselves. And I always thought to myself 'I can't really sit still for two hours, how would I do it for eternity and not get bored?' So when I found this path of Dhunami and I learned that I could not only be a conscious co-worker, but that I could choose and develop myself into the area of work that I wanted, I was pretty eager to get to it and to explore it. Every individual needs to make the choice for themselves, and that is the freedom that comes with this path, a spiritual freedom, a personal freedom, as well as a freedom that we give to all other Beings to make their own choices. Every individual has to determine, within themselves, what is right for them and what is not.

I'd like to talk here for a little while now on freedom. This is another subject that many people don't understand, and it can be quite difficult to explain. The first time an individual has a past life experience, or a Soul travel experience, the concept of freedom is immediately understood and known, even if there is no conscious realization or epiphany within the individual. The freedom that we are talking about here is in many aspects. First, it is a freedom from death, or rather the fear of death. When one has Soul-traveled, and has experienced the other worlds for him or herself, there is no fear left within that individual about dying, because one knows where he or she is going, what it is like on the other side, and how swiftly it is achieved. Also, when one steps on this path, whether he or she has had any kind of conscious traveling experience matters not because upon death of the physical body the Master is there, with that Soul, guiding him or her into the inner planes, the spiritual planes of existence.

It is also a freedom from the confines and limitations of the physical body. Since we can leave the body at our own volition, we can literally escape from the ordinary events of everyday life into the spiritual planes. Also, there have been many, many accounts of people saying either they left their bodies or they were taken out by the Masters so they would not have to consciously experience a traumatic event, such as a car accident, or injury, or a negative situation. These experiences can be read about in some of Darwin's books I believe, and the individual should trust this, because it is swifter than the mind can grasp. If the Master sees that you are going to be injured and you don't need to consciously experience that injury, then he will take you out of your body, and then put you back before you have realized what is happening. This is of course only if you are a chela of his and asked for his guidance and presence. The Master cannot come into your space, take you out of your body or guide you unless you have asked him to do so.

The freedom that a chela experiences in these teachings is freedom in Soul, freedom of body, freedom from fear, and all these things contribute to the freedom to really live life. So many people are so tense, stressed, have so many fears, concerns and questions about life; where they are going, why they are here, why they are in a present situation, what the future holds, among others. The spiritual and contemplative exercises in Dhunami allow the student to answer many of these questions for himself, and when we have these questions answered, we are more easy-going, more relaxed, and free from our minds and emotions, and thus able to live in the moment, which provides us a much more joyful, carefree, cheerful sort of existence.

As well as having this immense amount of freedom for ourselves, we allow others to be as well. We don't try to change people, or change the world. We don't go around telling others they are doing the wrong thing, or practicing the wrong beliefs, or damning them to hell. We allow others the freedom of life and the freedom of being. If someone asks a chela on this path why he is so happy, or carefree, that chela will share his knowledge and experiences, and that is all, we don't pressure anyone, or try to convince anyone, because we all should have the freedom to be who we want to be, and worship or not worship in the manner we choose, as long as it does not interfere with another person's space.

I cannot think of any aspect of life or spiritual life that the individual on this path does not have or lacks a greater freedom than his fellow man. If each individual were to open himself or herself to this Divine Spirit, and this Divine Love, you would soon find a greater life than you had previously known, and you would give your fellow man a greater amount of freedom and love than before, because you did not know it existed before. However, the individual should be aware that with this freedom comes a greater responsibility to the Sugmad, the Masters, and his fellow Beings.

Chapter Fifteen
April 21, 2008

All About Karma

Today I would like to discuss the topic of karma, which I have mentioned earlier, but neglected to explain in detail. Now karma is a very necessary part of our spiritual growth, in that we need to be able to work off our existing karma from this life as well as any past life karma the individual may have. In addition to this, we want to stop creating karma for ourselves so that we are not continually adding karma that needs to be worked off.

Our past life karma is that karma which we have developed over our previous lives, which can be from a number of things, it doesn't always have to be something drastic. When I am talking about past life karma, it could be something as simple as taking or keeping something that didn't belong to you, hating someone and constantly having negative thoughts and feelings about that person, being dishonest in our relationships with other people, and the list goes on. But what I am saying here is that just because you have past life karma does not mean you were a bad or terrible person. In fact, karma from past lives can include good karma, and indeed if the person is finding Dhunami in this life time, and considering stepping onto this path, one can be sure it is the good karma from past lives that has led him or her to this particular moment and this opportunity.

Now, this past life karma is something everyone has, and if you should like to find out more about it, you can do so by asking the Masters to show you. There have been many cases where individuals have had dreams or conscious experiences during their contemplative or spiritual exercises where the Master shows them that a particular person in their life, or a particular situation, is due to a karmic relation. Now, people already realize this, talk about it, and reference it without even thinking of it. People say, 'boy, I must have done something right to have so-and-so in my life, or to have this job that I have,' or whatever it may be. However, these people may not be recognizing that this karma goes much further than just this lifetime and can, in fact, go much further back than the previous lifetime. I have known individuals with karmic situations and relationships that spanned over four or five lifetimes, so this is something that the individual should and can get a handle on, and start to work through. As I said earlier, it can be shown to you which relationships and situations in your lifetime are karmic or have karmic ties, and you can see why, or what caused the karma, and you can see or know how far back it goes.

I want to assure the individual here that no matter how long it took for one to develop these karmic conditions, no matter how many lifetimes of karma are involved, if the chela takes up the study of Dhunami, and follows and surrenders to the Living Dhunami Master all of this karma will be worked out very quickly, as quickly as possible. I want to say here that just because we have karma with someone, and we are working it off in this lifetime, does not mean it cannot be a pleasant experience and a good relationship. It is all about our attitude, which is another thing that will have to be discussed. I know many individuals who come together in relationships because they had karma to work out from past lives, and they worked it off, and remained happily married. If you take the attitude that you're stuck with this person, or take the point of view that this is a negative situation, then it will be. But don't create that for yourself, because it does not have to be that way.

Now, we can help ourselves to work off this past life karma by doing things in the name of the Sugmad, for the Masters and for the Dhunami teachings. Every person who puts a brochure out, holds a class, gives a lecture or an introductory talk, or any other means of helping the Master in his mission to spread the knowledge of these teachings is working off past karma, as well as creating good or positive karma for himself for the future. This is why so many people see their lives start to change when they begin to give service to the Vi-Guru, the Living Dhunami Master of the Time, because he is working as swiftly as he possibly can to work out our karma, and every bit of help we of ourselves can do goes a long way.

The next thing I want to discuss here is our current karma, or our karma that we have created for ourselves in this lifetime. This also has to be paid off or worked off, and again the Living Dhunami Master of the Time and those of the Dhunami Order will help the individual in working off or getting rid of this karma, as long as we have asked. This current karma that we have created for ourselves, we often do when we are young. Very small children know the difference between right and wrong, because it is not always so much of a mental process, figuring it out, so to speak, but it is a feeling we get, inside ourselves when we are about to do something wrong and we know it. Many people call this instinct, or intuition, or conscience, but I call it Divine Spirit.

Now, this current life karma that we have to work off can usually be worked off quicker than the past life stuff, and we can often do this in the dream state. I know I preferred to work things out in the dream state rather than have to work them out here on this physical plane. All I had to do was ask the Master, and I was working off my karma and didn't even know it, most of the time. There is no reason for us to have to experience things here on this physical plane if we desire not to. This goes for past karma, as well as future situations.

Now again, we can help to work off this current life karma in the same way we are working off the past life karma, by giving of ourselves, our time, coin, our service in some manner to the Living Dhu-nami Master of the Time and these teachings. Now, the next thing the individual has to be aware of when it comes to karma, and working off karmic situations, is to prevent future karma or to stop creating karmic situations for ourselves. Once we understand how it works, there is no reason to continue to rack up karma against oneself, or what is called negative karma.

Now karma comes about, as I said before, because we have done something that we shouldn't have, taken something that wasn't ours or said or had negative thoughts or feelings about someone. The best way to prevent ourselves from racking up or causing negative karma for ourselves in the future is first and foremost to be honest. If we are honest with ourselves, with the Masters and Sugmad, then we cannot help but be honest with our fellow man. As long as we are honest, we will not create hardly any new karma for ourselves. There is a little saying Rebazar Tarzs told me, and I have written it in many places. It is one of the laws of the universe, that we should not do or say any-thing that is not true, kind, or necessary. Even though we are being honest with ourselves, and our fellowman, we can still think negative-ly, and react negatively, and this can cause karma for ourselves. Any-time we have a negative thought or feeling about another Being, whether it is our neighbor, the man on television, or one of the Mas-ters, that is a small bit of karma that will have to be worked out.

Practicing the presence of the Master, as well as chanting the holy words can help one to avoid this nasty business of negative karma. In addition, if the chela would do everything in the name of the Master, and surrender to the Master, then the Master will help us with these issues, and will catch us before we say or think something negatively, that would result in a karmic situation for ourselves. The Master upon initiating us has an obligation or responsibility and a duty to work to get us into the higher planes, and so he will work with us on every lit-tle thing, from the tiniest little thought to the biggest problems and or addictions, but only if we ask.

One finds that when the majority of karma has been worked out, and the individual has ceased his negative thoughts and feelings, and is thus free of future karma, life straightens out and many issues or obstacles disappear, life is more easy going for the individual, and he or she has less hassles and quarrels, and the Master asks very little in return for his service and gifts. May the Blessings be!

Chapter Sixteen
April 23, 2008

Power as Energy
360° Awareness

Tonight I would like to discuss energy. Divine Spirit is energy of ITself, and if one was able to capture IT and direct IT, we would be able to power all sorts of things, our houses, cars, various machines. Energy is sometimes used instead of the word power, but if the individual really thinks about it, these two ideas are the same thing, when we are talking about the energy or power to create or cause movement or action.

Now people who are on this path progressing rapidly or working off a great deal of karma, will sometimes feel tired, and they will wonder within themselves why they are so tired if they are in fact a vehicle for this Divine Spirit, this energy. It is because the Divine Spirit is working so quickly or efficiently within you and removing large areas that are blocking or hindering your spiritual growth. Now, this can only happen for a period of time and then Divine Spirit will go easy on the individual so to speak, so that he doesn't get out of balance. Sometimes when this happens, the individual wonders 'who turned off the flow' because they feel if they are not physically feeling tired or worn that the flow has decreased. This is not so. The flow of Divine Spirit will only decrease within an individual if he or she lowers themselves to a lesser plane than that to which they are developed. Even then, this flow doesn't decrease, per se, but the vibrations are lower, more harsh. I have spoken of this before, of an individual working from a lesser or lower plane than that which they are planted on or initiated into. This is their choice, but if they wish to continue progressing spiritually, they should get their attention and consciousness back up to the level it has been unfolded to.

Now Divine Spirit of ITself, being the essence of God, and energy or power, whichever you like to call IT, is able to clear out negative thought patterns, negative habits, as well as injuries and any other mental or physical situation one may be having. This energy, Divine Spirit, cannot be directed. All we can do is open ourselves to be a vehicle for IT. Some of the psychic energies on the lower planes can be used and manipulated, but I would not do that myself. I would not want the karma and responsibility that comes with an action such as that. The energy or power that is Divine Spirit is the most powerful substance that exists, and yet IT is the gentlest. Man does not always understand why things happen or why they are done a certain way, but you can be sure that if Divine Spirit is involved, and Divine Love is involved that whatever happens is for the good of the whole, the good of all individuals involved.

Now good is misinterpreted. When I say 'good' here, I mean in accordance with the spiritual awakening or spiritual development of society or the individual. Societies have cycles, just as nations do and man does, and I wrote quite a bit about that when I was here on this physical plane. Divine Spirit is not concerned with our material lives or our occupations, ITs purpose is to help individuals unfold themselves spiritually.

Now, once we step onto the path of Dhunami, and we are open to Divine Spirit and Divine Love, then every aspect of our lives will begin to get better, because when we have a developed or awakened awareness things become clear that puzzled us before, and this is true for our physical lives here as well. It is necessary for the individual to go slow with these teachings, because the Divine Spirit can be overwhelming; all that energy. If one desires to have power at all, and especially for their own selfish uses, they will surely be as far from IT as possible. However, if a person desires more of the Divine Spirit, this energy, this flow, for the benefit of all, he will surely and quickly have what he has asked for. Some people don't realize how much the Divine Spirit flows through each individual who is an open vehicle and how much IT will require of you when you begin to unfold to Self-realization.

I have spoken before about this nudging, when we are open to Divine Spirit and we are listening, we get all sorts of guidance coming through and occurring to our consciousness. Now sometimes even though the individual has asked for guidance, he will decide he wants to do his own thing, or sometimes doesn't want to listen to the guidance or direction that is given. When this happens, another nudge will be given, and sometimes even another if it is something very important or if the individual will be causing himself or putting himself in an unwanted situation unknowingly. But then that is all. It is up to the individual to listen to or to follow the guidance or not.

Now I would like to talk a little bit about developing one's awareness. Darwin spoke of this in his writings and I spoke about it as well. Ideally, we would like to have or develop ourselves to the point of 360° awareness. I know some of you may be wondering what this is, so I am going to explain it here, or attempt to. Sometimes we meet an individual, or we're talking with someone we know, and we can't seem to understand what this individual is talking about. Or you seem to understand a little, but can't see why the individual is thinking or feeling the way he or she is, and this is stated sometimes as not seeing where the person is coming from. This is because we have not developed ourselves to a degree that we are able to see or understand because perhaps we are only working with a 25° viewpoint, or a 50° viewpoint.

The higher we climb the spiritual ladder, the more expanded our consciousness and awareness becomes, and so we are able to understand our fellowman to a greater degree, or extent. This does not mean we always agree with them, or that we like what they are saying, but it simply means we will be able to understand what this individual is trying to communicate, and why he or she is thinking or feeling what they are communicating at that particular time. So many adverse effects happen due to miscommunication, especially in the workplace. Part of this is not listening or not taking the time to really think about or ask questions about what is being communicated, but it is also due to a lack of developing a wider awareness, going from maybe 75° to 100° in view and understanding.

Now developing our consciousness and our 360° viewpoint takes time, it will not happen overnight, and as just about any other spiritual quality it needs to be gradual, so as not to unbalance the individual. It is of a great advantage to the chela to see that this viewpoint is developed for a number of reasons. I have already explained the physical world benefits of such a quality, but also this helps the individual with his personal relationships on the physical as well as with work and in his endeavors.

Even greater than these benefits, or more important, is that if an individual is able to develop this viewpoint within himself or herself, then he or she will be able to see or judge better where they are working from spiritually, what they need to work on, and will be able to tell more readily when they have gotten out of balance, or are about to, or what could cause them to get out of balance. I know I talk a lot about balance and staying in balance, but that is because it is so important to one's spiritual growth.

Now if we have this desire within ourselves to unfold or expand our viewpoint, or our awareness to a greater degree, then we should ask the Masters for help with it, and then let it go. So many times individuals ask for help with an issue, or something that they need guidance on, and then don't let it go. They keep it in the mind area, and when that happens Divine Spirit and the Masters are unable to work on it, and unable to help the individual with it. I know it is difficult sometimes, this is something I struggled with as well, but sometimes we keep chewing it over because of a lack of trust in the Master or fear. If we release it, we will soon learn everything will be worked out, and we will have greater ease in letting go of things in the future.

Now, back to the expanded viewpoint. There are many reasons to keep journals or diaries on this path, and one of them is this very subject I have been discussing here. Sometimes we feel as though nothing has happened, that we have not changed, and that our awareness has not opened up or expanded even two degrees. If one was able to look back in a journal or diary, and see a year ago, even possibly six months ago, one would hardly recognize the person they used to be, or the viewpoint they used to have. This is even greater or better understood when we go back two years, or even five years, we are able to see a gradual progression and unfolding of the state of awareness or consciousness simply by our thoughts, feelings, actions and how we interact with the world.

Now I stated before that expanding our awareness helps with many aspects of life, and one I forgot to discuss is our reactions. Our reactions are important, and I will discuss them in greater detail later, but this expanding of viewpoint, awareness, or consciousness helps us with our reactions to other individuals. If we are talking with someone, and we don't understand what the person is saying or why they feel that way, sometimes we can become angry or frustrated with that person, and this is an unnecessary reaction, and one we should not fall into. Ask yourself, 'what is the point in getting hot and bothered about this individual's thoughts or feelings?' When we have developed our viewpoint to 100° or 200°, we are able to simply look at that individual and say or think to ourselves, 'well, that's just where that person is right now,' or, 'that's just where that individual is working from right now,' and we are able to leave it at that. This helps us tremendously in staying in balance, not reacting emotionally and lowering our own vibrations, as well as allowing us to still have goodwill and Divine Love for this individual. This developed awareness, in my opinion, is one of the greatest things an individual can do for himself.

Chapter Seventeen
April 24, 2008

Being Cause
Aspects of Divine Love

I was discussing reactions before, and saying that we shouldn't be reacting certain ways to certain situations. Many people do not understand the cause and effect law, which is also called the Law of Karma. Now the law of cause and effect simply states that when we perform an action, we are setting in motion a series of events which will eventually come back to us, no matter if the starting action or cause is good or bad. Many people will understand this as the scientific law that I believe Newton put down, that for every action there is an equal and opposite reaction. This is somewhat similar to what I am talking about here. Every action we take is either a cause or an effect. Now when we are reacting to someone, whether we get angry or yell, or what have you, we are being the result of their action or their thoughts. This can set into motion a karmic tie with that person, or with others we come into contact with regarding this situation.

Now what I want to say here is this: If we are always acting as cause, we are not taking on anymore karma, nor are we being the effect of anyone else's. When we have a reaction to something someone else does, no matter how large or small our reaction, we are putting ourselves in an unnecessary situation, and we may be getting ourselves tangled up in their karma or creating karma with them, that we do not want to have to pay back. Many people have a misunderstanding of this law, for various reasons. They think, 'how can I not react to things,' because they think this means any reaction at all will cause karmic involvement. This is not true. If we head out the door in the morning and we have goodwill for our fellowman and we keep that attitude or outlook all day, regardless of what happens, we will be in good shape. We can even share in our fellowman's grief or sadness, briefly, or be compassionate and sympathetic, but again, only for a moment. It is very good and healthy to be friendly and sup- portive, and let your friends, co-workers and family know you care about them. The area where the individual can get into a bit of trouble is when we allow ourselves to be drawn or pulled into a negative area by those around us. Soul is a happy Being, and when we are in a negative area, very sad or upset or angry, we cannot be acting in Soul, and so we are operating from the lower worlds and from the lower self. When we do this, we are liable to get ourselves in a bit of trouble or cause some karma for ourselves.

Another area the individual can have some trouble with is to get angry. I understand this is a tough one to keep a handle on and I have had my share of angry moments. What we need to remember here is that when we act in anger, and we yell or shout or other things, these things are sure to come back to us, at times when we could surely do without it. When we react to something in anger, we are being the effect of whatever it was that made us angry and getting ourselves involved in that karma.

Now I want to state here that anger is very different from being firm, assertive, and not letting people walk over you. I will always give it to you straight and so will any other Master you meet because knowing the Laws of the Universe, the Law of Cause and Effect, and the Law of Karma, there is no other way a Master can be, no other way but honest and straightforward. I encourage each one of you to implement this thinking, this belief of honesty and being forthright into your daily lives. Because here's the thing, there's no reason to get all tangled up and involved in some karmic situation that is not yours and that you have no business being a part of. We work very hard, and the Masters work very hard with us to get rid of our karma from the moment we step on the path, and we need to be careful and conscientious as to what we are getting ourselves into so to speak. If one desires to know more about cause and effect and karma, a study of it can be done at the Temple Within or in Darwin's books as well as my older books.

A good way to stay away from getting involved in karma or getting wrapped up in a situation that isn't ours to get into is to constantly evaluate and ask ourselves: 'where am I working from, what area of the inner worlds am I dwelling in consciousness at this moment?' If you are angry or feeling fear or hatred, you can bet it is one of the lower worlds. The higher worlds contain Divine Love, which also encompasses those positive or helpful feelings, giving someone a pat on the back for a good job, and this is why this sort of exchange is good and is encouraged. This will not get the individual into trouble as far as cause and effect or karma are concerned. But it needs to be an every moment, in this moment thing, because that negativity, that anger, can sneak up on us and can be causing us to react before we even know we are reacting; even for those of you who are higher initiates, you still need to be aware of it and cautious of it.

When we are being cause, we are being individuals working from the highest area open to us in the spiritual planes, but when we are being the effect and we are reacting, especially in a negative manner, then we are subjecting ourselves to the lowest of the inner planes, and there is no reason to ever do that to ourselves. If each person would put just a little attention on this subject for a few weeks, one would soon find that a check system grows into place and before we know it we are automatically checking or recognizing where we are working from, thus preventing ourselves from engaging in any karmic activity, or negativity I should say. It takes just a little time and patience and a bit of help from the Masters, but it is a quality or ability that is extremely useful for our daily lives as well as our spiritual growth.

I would like to speak a little bit about Divine Love now. Most people have difficulty imagining what Divine Love is or feels like. It takes some time to develop ourselves to the degree that we are receiving a good amount of Divine Love, and only then does an individual usually gain an understanding of what it is. It is necessary for each and every individual to develop a love within themselves, a Divine and pure love, because this is needed before we can enter into the higher spiritual planes.

I spoke earlier about filling ourselves with love in order to receive love or get more love. This Divine Love that I am speaking of is very different from the love we feel for our family and friends. However, if we were to employ Divine Love in every aspect of our lives, our relationships with our family and friends would improve and would be greater relationships with a greater love and understanding for one another. This is often what man calls or thinks of as true love because this Divine Love is pure and true since it derives from and flows out from the Sugmad. It encompasses the feelings of sincerity, honesty, sympathy, as well as compassion and kindness.

Now people usually try to work on having these aspects of Divine Love instead of focusing on or trying to get Divine Love itself. This can be very difficult, time consuming, and frustrating for the individual. This is just like the man who seeks all that God is when he should simply be seeking God Itself. If one would ask for Divine Love in their lives instead of working on each little aspect of IT, one would have much more success with the matter, would save himself a lot of time, energy, concern, and frustration as well as despair. Any individual can contemplate on Divine Love to gain a greater understanding of it.

Now, I should take the time here to explain what contemplation is. When we have a question or a desire within ourselves to learn about something or know something we can contemplate on it. This is where we sit down, relax and quiet ourselves, and begin to chant either HU or our own word, the Master's name, or any other word from the higher planes. We do this only a few times, perhaps 4 to 6. Then we should ask our question, or state we desire to know more about Divine Love or whatever it is we are looking for, and wait. Take deep breaths and focus on your breathing trying to keep your mind free from thoughts and images, other than the blue or white Light or the Master's gaze or face. After a few minutes the individual can begin to chant again, about 4-6 times, and then again wait for an answer. This is very difficult for some individuals when they first try because they find it so difficult to quiet the mind. I suggest trying some of the other techniques, the spiritual exercise techniques, as well as the relaxation techniques laid out in this book if you are experiencing difficulty in turning off the mind.

Now we may get our answer the first time we ask, we may get it after the second set of chants, and we may not. I don't recommend going more than 3 or 4 times with the chants and breathing. Sometimes we have to give it time, and sometimes we have to unfold to a greater degree before we can experience or know that which we are seeking.

Now this substance that is Divine Love flows out from the Living Dhunami Master as well as the other Masters and touches all those he comes into contact with either on the spiritual planes or this physical plane. We are each one of us an individual Soul, a spark of Spirit, a drop of the Sugmad. If we can see ourselves and those around us in this manner, and really try to develop seeing people this way, we will know Divine Love and be a vehicle for IT. This is sometimes called seeing the individual or seeing people in the heart of the Sugmad if we can visualize them or know they are a part of the Divine. If the Sugmad and the Masters and the Living Dhunami Master can see each individual with great love and as a Being from the Sugmad, or a part of IT then we can see them as such as well.

Now Jesus spoke of this when he said, 'love thy neighbor as thyself.' This puzzled many people but if one begins to see every person they meet as a part of the Sugmad, just as we ourselves are, then our daily lives would be filled with Divine Love, laughter, joy, and good will.

Now having Divine Love does not mean you are going to like everybody or that you have to. It doesn't mean you have to agree with everyone or that you have to go out and volunteer or work in charities. It simply means that we have largely eliminated the negativities within ourselves as far as anger, hatred, fear, resentment and others and that we give each and every person the freedom, respect, and detached love that they are entitled to as individual Souls.

That is another thing I'd like to talk about: This Divine Love is often described as detached love, and it is. This simply means that we give the individual the freedom to live. Many times we see people, especially parents, who are always trying to direct their children, always trying to tell them what to do, no matter how old they get. Now some of this is very helpful and constructive, but only to an extent. There comes a point in that child's life when the parent needs to step back and simply give the child Divine Love, wishing them good will, the best, and all that, but allowing the person to make their own decision, and not getting bent out of shape about it because we think we know what is best.

Divine Love is the highest expression of love that exists because we must allow individuals their own freedom to do as they will. Otherwise, we can get into an area of trouble and possibly control issues. Now this Divine Love, even though it is a detached love, is still a much warmer, giving, and accepting love than what man thinks of as love. It is not cold or insensitive as some think. This Divine Love is also a great vehicle or carrier for forgiveness. Many people have problems with this subject of forgiveness and many people hang on to feelings or situations for years and years. If we would fill ourselves with Divine Spirit and Divine Love and allow it to flow through us, it will remove all that negativity and leave us with forgiveness, gratitude, and understanding. I could spend years and years talking about Divine Love and write many books on the subject, but as with many spiritual things, the individual needs to experience it for him or herself to really know what I am communicating here. Give it a try, what have you got to lose?

Chapter Eighteen
April 25, 2008

Choosing a Path of Our Own
Being Bold and Adventuresome
The Gaze of the Master

W hen I first began to search for God, when I was a young man, I really had a very limited concept of what I was looking for. Some of you who are reading this book will feel like it is speaking directly to your Soul, and that this material is very familiar, and in large part you agree with what is being said here. Others will read this and perhaps dismiss it altogether, and some of you will wonder about it, maybe try a technique or two that I have laid out here for you, and question within yourself the validity or reality of what I am saying. Whichever road or path the individual takes is the one that is right for that particular individual at this particular time. We should never feel like we have to hurry to find God or Self-realization, or heaven, and we should never follow a path simply because we feel there is nothing else out there that fulfills us. Sometimes the best way to find the right path that suits us is to stop looking and stop trying. This is the surrender I was talking about earlier, and this pertains to every single aspect of one's life, both inner and outer.

We do not want chelas living double lives, so to speak, that they practice one thing on the inner, or for their spiritual lives, and then try to do another, or practice something else in their physical lives. Dhunami is a way of life; it is not a religion, or a philosophy, so to speak. We call it a spiritual path, but really Dhunami is just the tool we use to travel the spiritual path, so this line of teachings can only be called a way of life. I've heard people refer to Sunday Christians and I suppose they have those sort of sayings for all religions, of the people who go through the motions, do their weekly or daily activity, and then go about their way, not really applying or living the religion or path they are following. If one tries to do this with Dhunami, they will have very little to no success in either parts of their lives, the inner or the outer, because it is impossible to do such a thing. Every aspect of our lives, every event that takes place, every moment, can be and is a spiritual event or moment.

I wrote about this before. I believe in one of my books I stated that when we have developed ourselves to the point that we can recognize the spiritual aspects and recognize the miracles that are happening to us constantly, we will begin to feel complacent and think or feel those miracles are commonplace. There is a spiritual aspect or spiritual viewpoint that one can take, and it takes time to develop it, but once we do, we no longer see ourselves as having two separate lives, an inner and an outer life. We have only or we live only on the inner, and focus on or view things from the spiritual worlds, and everything else, all this physical world stuff is just events and things that help us learn our spiritual lessons and allow us to do our spiritual work.

People who think this idea of me dictating a book is too far-fetched, or the idea of having communication with Spiritual Masters and Travelers is too extraordinary or fantastic to believe, are people who are not open to looking at the world from the spiritual perspective. They view the world only by the laws and rules that they are familiar with here on this physical plane of existence. These rules are typically what we have learned from our parents, from grade school, high school, and college, and usually are based on the accepted laws of science at the particular time. If one looks through history and looks at the accepted ideas and rules for different periods of time, there has been an expansion of awareness and an expansion of consciousness. Man used to think the world was flat, then it was generally accepted that the world was round, but that the earth was the center of the universe, and everything else rotated around it. Then we learned that wasn't the case. In every generation or every time period, we are able to learn more about the world around us, and therefore about ourselves.

So here is the point I am trying to make: Conventional society may not believe in Spiritual Masters, or dictation from them, or contemplative exercises, but society and its general concepts are often mistaken. In almost every part of history ,we can see a situation where society generally believed one thing and maybe one or a few people believed something different. These people were outcasts, until someone was finally able to prove they were right all along, and society had the wrong idea. If we were to develop that spiritual perspective, that concept of viewing things from the spiritual aspect, we would find many explanations, answers, and events in our lives that many people would dismiss, simply because we have been so indoctrinated that the world is a certain way.

People who wonder about what new technology will be developed or what the new space program is going to find, these are the curious, and the bold, and the adventuresome. These are the people who will be able very quickly to look within themselves for spiritual experiences, and have them. For others, it takes what I call a little breaking up of thought patterns, and this just means that some of our old ways of thinking have to be forgotten and tossed out before we can entertain or experience new ones. This is why an open mind is really the first step, because sometimes it takes a little while to forget the things we've been so accustomed to or to open ourselves to something we would have thought or think is impossible. In Divine Spirit, nothing is impossible, and each person can experience that for themselves.

It is time to talk about the Darshan. I don't think I have mentioned this aspect of the teachings or the Living Dhunami Master of the Time in this book so far. I wrote about it in my early books, and Darwin talked about it a decent amount. The Darshan is a very important part of the teachings for the chela and for the newcomer. This is another reason we need the Living Dhunami Master. The Darshan or a Darshan is the gaze of the Living Dhunami Master, one who has the Light of God and the higher spiritual planes flowing from his eyes. This is a great amount of love, energy, and warmth, as well as spiritual knowledge. The Darshan is usually given at the time of the initiation or preceding an initiation. It is first given to a person just stepping onto this path, and it usually brings about a great spiritual realization within the individual. For the new person, it is a way to get connected to or linked up with the Light, the flow of Divine Spirit, and the Master and the teachings. Anyone who is fortunate enough to receive such a gift should know they are well blessed and are on the path to realization. Anytime a student wishes or desires, he or she can call upon any of the Masters of the Dhunami Order for an experience. One should understand these Beings in the spiritual planes are very busy, and it may take some time before they have a free moment to work with us.

The Darshan can be given on the inner or on the outer. Some people have told stories of going to seminars or events and wanting the Darshan, wanting the Living Dhunami Master of the Time to gaze into their eyes and begin the awakening of the true Self, the Soul, but he avoids their gaze. He will only give the Darshan to those who are spiritually ready and in need of it. And those who are clamoring after it are sure to have to wait. Many people report healings after experiencing the Darshan from the Living Dhunami Master of the Time and various other miraculous happenings that are common in Dhunami.

The purpose of the Darshan is to uplift the individual and link him or her up with Divine Spirit and eventually the Sound current. I talked about the Light and Sound earlier, and those who hear any Sound should also be aware they are very blessed. I can remember some gentleman thinking there was something wrong with his ears, because he was hearing a high pitched buzzing noise, but it was really his inner ears hearing the sweet sounds of the spiritual planes.

The Darshan is just one way the Living Dhunami Master of the Time exposes us to more of the Divine Spirit, or gets us connected to IT. He also works to develop the chela's tisra til, or spiritual eye, so that the Light can be seen during contemplation, as well as the spiritual ears so the Sound can be heard. The Master gives us so many tools to help us in our spiritual development they are too many to list, but he will never of himself advertise this or say these things about himself.

There are many spiritual laws that man does not know of, or understand. Most of them really are the most basic laws one can think of, such as 'do unto others as you would have done to you.' This is talking about the law of karma because that which we do to others we must pay for in some manner according to the law of karma. There are many examples of this. When the chela finally steps on the path of these teachings and makes a study of the laws, he or she will notice that they were already aware of these laws, perhaps not exactly as they are stated in my writings and Darwin's writings, but that they are familiar with the laws. We do not require or ask anything extravagant or extraordinary. We don't expect people to act as saints, or as society thinks saints act. There are a few simple laws we talk about, but again it is up to the individual if he wishes to make an effort in abiding by these laws. His life would sure be easier, simpler, and smoother if he did. Anyone who desires to learn more about these laws and how they can affect our lives can do so at the Temple Within.

Now I want to tell you that these laws were not set down by me, but are the simplest laws from the Sugmad that have been known since the beginning of man's civilization. Everything the Masters have done, and do, and will do is for the benefit of the individual who seeks God and the spiritual advancement of the whole, and that is all.

Chapter Nineteen
April 26, 2008

A Talk on Self-Realization

T his evening I am going to discuss the topic of Self-realization. I talk about this often, as did Darwin in his writings, but some people may be a little confused. First, I would like to say that one begins Self-realization upon entering the Soul plane after or during the Soul initiation, which is the last initiation to be done on the physical plane in these teachings.

Now when I say Self-realization, most people are thinking I am talking about or what is going to happen is a sudden awakening, like all of a sudden someone turned on the lights, but that is not usually how it goes. The awakening of the individual must be gradual, so that the person stays in a balanced state and is able to adjust to the new vibrations and new laws or rules of the plane.

Now, anytime the individual receives an initiation the flow of Divine Spirit gets more and more subtle even though it is increasing. Everything else gets more subtle as well, as far as our own awakenings, or realizations, our issues or habits we are trying to get rid of, as well as the experiences we have in the spiritual worlds. I don't want people to think that they have to work real hard to get into the Soul plane and then that's it, job's over, because that is just not the case. When one is able to receive the Soul initiation, that individual has earned the right to enter into that plane. It does not necessarily mean they will have overnight Self-realization or that our spiritual work or search is over, or that we have reached a level of perfection and negativity cannot reach us any longer.

These are all common misconceptions that I want to clear up right now. It takes time to develop Self-realization, and self-awareness, and this should be done gradually and slowly. One will begin to see changes in the way he views the world and himself, but it will be gradual so as not to upset the delicate balance within man. After entering the Soul plane, one will begin to recognize such traits within himself as selflessness, general joy and happiness, a greater level of Divine Love and Divine Spirit, a truthfulness and a higher degree of ethics and morals than can be taught, and letting go of the mind and its worries and the selfish desires of the little self within man. There are many more than this and as I stated previously this is a wonderful time for a person to keep a journal, and over a period of 6 months to a year, one will hardly recognize who he was previously.

Now, people begin to think that once they have reached the Soul plane and have a level of Self-realization and awareness that their spiritual work is over, but it really is just the opposite. Once an individual has reached this level of spiritual development, he begins to realize a desire to help his fellow man to achieve what he has achieved for himself. A desire to serve the Sugmad, the Masters, and his fellow man awakens within the individual, and he may find himself hanging posters, holding classes, or helping with Dhunami events, which he may have had no desire to do in the past. In addition to the outer work, the individual is often given work on the inner, sometimes it is just helping his family and friends with their spiritual development and issues, but it can cover a huge variety of jobs or work or service, however one likes to say it.

So really when one looks at it from this perspective, the spiritual work has just begun. Once the individual has developed himself into the higher worlds above the Soul plane, he will begin to be shown various areas of work he or she could enter into and eventually the individual must pick an area to work in, at least for a period of time.

The next point I'd like to discuss is that sometimes when a person reaches the Soul plane and has their initiation, they think they have reached a level of perfection or a level of superiority. This is not the case. In fact, a person who is spiritually advanced or dwells within the higher planes must be very careful and watchful, because if they let even a small piece of the ego or Kal into their lives they could cause themselves to dwell in, or have their consciousness in the lower worlds. The higher one goes the more careful and aware one needs to be, asking themselves always if they are being a clear open vehicle for Divine Spirit, or if they are working from the lower worlds. It is sometimes easier for a higher initiate to become wrapped up in the mental or emotional world and sometimes they have trouble seeing their way out of it. It takes time to raise their consciousness back to the level it was before, as high as it can possibly be based on that individual's unfoldment. When one is dwelling in a physical body, there can be no perfection, for only in Soul is such a thing possible.

Another thing I would like to clear up here is that a person dwelling in the higher states of consciousness in the higher spiritual planes can still be sad, they can still grieve and they can still feel depression and lethargy. However, should the individual continue his spiritual and contemplative exercises, he will be able to overcome such feelings very quickly and it will not be as bad or to such a degree that a person without spiritual development or spiritual awakening will experience. But I really want to drive home here the point that those dwelling in these higher planes are not perfect, they are not above anyone or better than anyone, nor are they invincible or incapable of error, being incorrect, or dwelling in the lower worlds. These people are human and they can make what man calls mistakes just like any other living Being.

Self-realization is really the first step toward God-realization. When we first step onto this path and we have our first initiation, which usually consists of the Darshan, that is the first step in our journey to Self-realization and awareness. That being said, when we finally achieve Self-realization, that is our first step toward God-realization, which should be our ultimate goal in this lifetime. I think that is enough for tonight.

Chapter Twenty
April 30, 2008

Pulling Divine Spirit into Your Life

The type of attitude has yet to be discussed and it is a very important topic, one that we should all be well aware of and educated about. Now, I want to talk here mostly about positive and negative attitudes. A person who has a positive attitude in life will go volumes farther than someone who has a very negative attitude. Sometimes it is very difficult to tell where we are working from, or if we have a positive or negative attitude. An easy way to determine this is what man calls optimism. If one has the outlook that no matter what happens or what one does, it will not turn out well, that is a negative attitude. However, if one is able to say to themselves 'maybe this will work,' or, 'I'll give it a shot,' one can and will have greater experiences.

Now some people think a positive outlook is simply having an open mind and to an extent this is true. If we have a negative attitude or outlook on life, we aren't open to the possibility of a positive outcome. Our attitudes shape our thoughts and feelings. I am not saying we should expect the best in every situation, or think that nothing wrong is going to happen because sometimes things happen.

I remember a young woman who had a car accident, I believe Darwin wrote about this, and this young woman was very upset, saying that this should not have happened to her and it was a big inconvenience, and this and that. Another young man had also had an automobile accident, but he was thankful he was not hurt, there was minimal damage to his car, and he found a great mechanic for future use. These two people have such a huge difference in attitude. The young woman is looking at everything from a negative perspective, whereas the young man is able to see things from a more positive outlook.

Most every situation or event in our lives can be looked at with a positive attitude, and we can find something good about it or something we have learned from it. If we are able to do this or if we put forth an effort to do this, we are able to grow by leaps and bounds, because we are learning and being grateful and thankful and filled with love. By having a positive attitude, we are placing our attention on the positive aspects of life, including Divine Spirit. The more we put our attention on something, the more we are able to surround ourselves with it, recognize it, and have more of it in our lives. So, by having a positive attitude we are really just pulling or attracting the Divine Spirit into our lives.

Now with Divine Spirit comes the Light and Sound to guide us, as well as the Living Dhunami Master, and before we know it we have or are on the path to progressing spiritually. Darwin wrote volumes about this when he was on this physical plane, because it is so very important to our spiritual growth. If we are always looking for the negative or seeing things from a negative perspective, then that is what is drawn to us, that is what we attract into our lives. It has been stated that in order to get love you must give love, and the same is true with Divine Spirit or the positive aspects of life. It is the same thing. If one wishes to have the positive force or aspect of Divine Spirit, we must give forth or look at things from that perspective. There are many ways to say it and it has been stated many ways, but man needs to realize that the only way to improve his present situation, both physical and spiritual, is to have a positive attitude to bring the Divine Spirit into one's life, as well as the Living Dhunami Master.

If man could understand that many things occurring in his life are opportunities, instead of seeing them as negative events, then he would be much better off and would possibly learn more about himself as a Spiritual Being. Now as I said before people sometimes have difficulty in discerning their own attitude, or whether they are having a positive or negative outlook. There are many ways to determine this. I have stated so many times that individuals should keep a journal and this is another reason why. If we can look back at an event that happened or our views about something a couple weeks or a month ago, we can get a pretty good idea of where our attention is, if it is on the negative or the positive aspects of life. Try to listen to yourself more. Think about what you are saying and why you are thinking or saying it. If we would examine ourselves more closely and determine our reasons or motives for certain actions, thoughts and feelings, we would save ourselves a great deal of complications, sorrows, and frustrations. And I say this because if we are acting or speaking out of jealousy, hatred or anger, and we say or do something we wouldn't otherwise, then we are liable to cause some problems for ourselves. If we would keep a handle on our attitudes and our outlook, keeping them positive and filled with love and Divine Spirit, then we would be calmer, happier individuals with less troubles, worries, and problems.

Chapter Twenty-One
May 4, 2008

The Neutral Zone

I have talked often in this book about having an open mind. Many people think they have an open mind but are really only fooling themselves. It is a hard one to recognize and to keep after. It does need to be kept after though, because even though we may have an open mind about one thing or one particular subject does not mean we are open about another.

Now, truly having an open mind means we are neither for nor against anything. Darwin wrote this many times. I want to set the record straight that this does not mean we are lacking opinions or likes or dislikes. We can enjoy our club soda or steak, we can cheer for the ball team, and we can drive a certain car, whatever we like. What I am talking about here is when a person says, 'well that is just wrong.' Blanket statements are not the way of the individual with an open mind. The individual would be better off taking the stance of 'well, this is what is right for me. Doesn't mean it is right for everybody or anybody else, but it is the right thing for me.' A clear example of this is vegetarianism. Now you'll meet many people who will say all people should be vegetarians but this is just not true because some people due to their chemical structure need to have animal protein to feel good, have energy, and be able to fulfill their responsibilities. That being said, some people digest meat poorly and are better off on a vegetarian diet.

Now I know this may seem like a trivial example, but it needs to be simple when we start to talk about religion or politics. People sometimes have a difficult time of understanding how we as people can have such different views and ideas. The example of type of diet should be applied to all aspects of one's life because we must be open, understanding, and flexible, but we must also know that which is right for ourselves. Anytime an individual gets into an area of being for or against anything, Divine Spirit is unable to show the person the best route or course of action for themselves. Let me put it this way; if we ask our neighbor what the weather is going to be tomorrow, but we already have our mind made up that it is going to be sunny, when he replies that it will rain we don't pay any attention to him.

Another way to look at this is people who don't believe in Spiritual Beings or Spiritual planes and then wonder why they can't have a spiritual experience. They are keeping themselves from it. Rebazar Tarzs stated this to me when he said, 'you, yourself are the problem,' or something to that effect. Now I know I am using a lot of examples here, but sometimes that is the best way to understand what is being communicated. If a person has a strong feeling about something or has an opinion about it, has their mind already made up about it, then that individual has closed himself off to all other possibilities I remember a young man once who wanted a certain type of car, he researched that car, he collected photographs of it, and he imagined himself driving it, and didn't consider any other type of car. Well, he sat down to have a contemplation about which car he should buy and he kept looking for this particular car and because he was looking for that car, that's what he saw. Now this was his imagination mind you, not Divine Spirit. We can always tell when it is Divine Spirit because we get the feeling of Divine Love with it.

Anyway, so this young man went out and bought this car and every day he had a new problem with it and he got very angry. He began to get upset with Divine Spirit because he thought Divine Spirit had mis-led him. Well, now that his infatuation with this car he had wanted so badly was over and he wasn't thinking about it anymore, didn't have any opinions or feelings about it one way or the other, well don't you know it, that's just when in contemplation he saw a totally different car, one he would never have considered. And so he went in and traded in the car he got before, the one he wanted, and got himself an older model of this car Divine Spirit had shown him, when he was finally open to receiving some information about it. Well, this man had that car that Divine Spirit showed him for a very long time and never had a day of trouble with it.

My point here is this: Divine Spirit and the Masters want to help us in our daily lives and they will answer any questions we ask of them and give us any kind of information we want, but we have to be open to it, and receptive to it. We can't simply say, 'Divine Spirit, tell me to buy this particular car or go to this particular school,' because this is not allowing ourselves to be guided, this is simply looking for confir-mation or wanting someone to tell us that we are right. In order to get an answer or the information we are looking for, we must be indiffer-ent to what the answer will be. We must not have any feelings one way or the other about it in order to receive the truth. That is why so many answers and so many spiritual experiences come when we stop looking for them, when we cease to have any feeling about them or desire for them.

Now, I know it is difficult sometimes, especially when we have an emotional reaction to something or when we have had an experience in the past. I was saying the other day that we need to constantly ask ourselves 'why am I thinking or feeling this way, why am I acting or reacting this way.' Well, this is a perfect tool to use here as well, be-cause if we can recognize we have an emotional feeling about some-thing or we have a strong feeling about something, then we are able to say to ourselves 'well gee, maybe I should open myself up about this.' We can recognize that we are not basing our actions or feelings on Divine Spirit, which we should always try to do. It won't steer us wrong in any situation as long as we are open to the direction. Sometimes the best thing we can do for ourselves is to forget about it for a while, put it away, and go on to something else. If we desire to be open and we declare ourselves open vehicles for Divine Spirit daily, then we can know or better recognize when we are being closed-minded about a subject.

I want to say here that many individuals have passed up opportunities for physical and spiritual growth because they were closed-minded and this is a shame. This is another area we have to keep after because we're going along fine, being open, getting our answers and then suddenly we are confronted with something we have a strong feeling about. If we would recognize it as an opportunity to open ourselves to Divine Spirit, open our minds, our viewpoints, and our awareness, we will be guided and shown what is right for us as individuals every time. This book is a perfect example. Many people will be immediately opposed to it, not even willing to be open-minded, neutral, or have no strong feeling about it one way or another. These people will not be able to get an answer from Divine Spirit or the Masters about it, and in my opinion when they do that to themselves, they are really missing out in life and on opportunities.

Chapter Twenty-Two

May 5, 2008

Managing the Kal
Faith, Trust and Spiritual Protection

I would like to talk tonight about the Kal. I have talked in this book a great deal about the Kal, usually warning people against this force. I think I need to say some other things about it. Now any individual that steps onto this path and feels like they need to fear the Kal or be afraid of the Kal is mistaken. We never have any reason to fear. When we fear something, we are putting attention on it, and when we do this, as I explained before, we can draw that very thing to ourselves by focusing on it. This is why I stated before that the individual should put his attention on Divine Spirit.

Now, we also should not fear the Kal because once we have stepped on this spiritual path and we have accepted the Living Dhunami Master as our spiritual guide, then we have a level of spiritual protection. That is not to say that the Kal is unable to trip us up, to get us riled up or to bring out some anger we may have, but if the individual recognizes this, and learns from it, then we should be thankful that we have learned a lesson and that we have been shown something that could possibly hold us back in our spiritual growth. I stated before that this physical world is a training ground for all Souls, and if

119

we can look at the Kal as one who administers tests, much like the Masters do sometimes to see if we are ready for the next step, then we are having a positive attitude and we will find very little throws us off balance or keeps us from progressing.

I have stated before, and Darwin put it to music, that the dark threads, meaning the Kal, are as needful as the threads of gold and silver, the Dhunami Masters and Divine Spirit, because in this lower world, we need to constantly be aware of where we are working from and if we are filled with Divine Spirit. The Kal, in a way, does us a favor when he tests us and when he tries to get us to feel angry, or react. He is teaching us, although it is a very different way than the Masters do, which is always with Divine Love.

Now I know some people are going to read this and think, 'boy this must be the Kal speaking,' but all I am doing here is to give the individual a positive helpful outlook for their spiritual growth, as well as eliminate their fear, as well as take their attention away from the Kal. Don't misunderstand what I am saying here; the Kal is the negative force, but it was put into the lower worlds by the Sugmad to help purify man and help him progress spiritually so that he may become a coworker with the Sugmad.

Now I mentioned earlier the spiritual protection one has from the Living Dhunami Master and this is on the physical as well as the spiritual planes. There are many people who have called on the Living Dhunami Master during a nightmare and they were taken out of that situation. There are many people who were taken out of their bodies when a nasty event or injury was going to happen. This is the protection I am talking about. Do not expect the Master to shield you or protect you from the experiences you must have and the lessons you must learn for your spiritual development, whether these lessons are learned through the Master himself or the Kal. Because, we can sit here and say, 'oh that nasty Kal, what a terrible thing' or we can say, 'I'm thankful for the experiences so that I can learn, grow and maintain a balance within myself.'

I suppose this is the philosophy of the father who throws their child into the lake or pool so they will learn to swim. We can sit back, always afraid of what might happen, or we can go out into life and if our doggie paddle isn't doing the trick then we can switch to the breast stroke. I hope you catch my meaning with this. Only by getting into life, getting into the teachings and having experiences can one ever learn or make any bit of progress towards our spiritual goals. Once we step on this path, the Masters are always with us and Divine Spirit always surrounds us, so we need never fear anything. If we are open to this Divine Spirit and the Living Dhunami Master at every moment of our lives, which takes practice, It will tell us when we are getting a little out of balance, when we are being angry, or when we are being confronted with the Kal. We should never worry about these things, for if we do, it means we are not listening to the Masters or Divine Spirit or that we do not trust the Masters or Divine Spirit. It takes time, I understand, to shed that worry and negativity, but one soon finds a little bit of faith in these teachings goes a very long way.

Chapter Twenty-Three
May 16, 2008

Recognizing the Living Dhunami Master
Discerning a True Spiritual Experience
Look to the Source

N ow, I want to talk a little more about the Living Dhunami Master, or the Living Dhunami Master of the Time, however you like to say it. Many people wonder, with so many individuals claiming to be Masters, or claiming that they can give people spiritual upliftment, how one is to discern who is truly the Living Dhunami Master of the Time. I admit this can sometimes become a struggle within an individual, especially if the individual takes it into the emotional or mental area. What I mean by this is when an individual tries to determine the Master based on their emotional feelings about this individual. For example, one person says to him/herself 'well, it can't be Mr. So-and-so, because one day I was passing him on the street and I thought he was a little short with me, so it couldn't be him.' People want to look at all types of emotional interactions and determine, or ask themselves 'would a Spiritual Master act like that?' Or people try to take it into the mental area and analyze this person's behaviors, his personal life, and his history with the teachings. Many people take this way too far and think that if a person ever made a bad decision or what man calls a mistake, that this individual couldn't possibly be the Living Dhunami Master.

Well, I've got news for you. The Living Dhunami Master is human, just like everyone else, and he's had his spiritual lessons to learn just like everyone else. We cannot judge a person by the actions they have done in the past. This is not living in the moment, which is so very necessary if we are going to dwell in the pure positive areas. Now there are many things an individual can get hung up on, so to speak, when looking at a person and trying to tell if they are the Living Dhunami Master. Going into the emotional and mental area, I already discussed. This also includes judging his personality. We should never think, 'well, he's too quiet,' or, 'he's not well known,' or, 'he's not very personable,' because the Living Dhunami Master always has the qualities that the majority of people in that society have and he always has the qualities that will best suit him in bringing forth Dhunami.

So, now that we know what types of judgments or methods we should avoid in determining a true Spiritual Master, I'm going to tell you the only ways you can. A real Spiritual Master radiates Divine Spirit and Divine Love. When you get around this person, when you think about this person and when you look at his picture, as long as you have an open mind and heart, you will have a feeling of joy, warmth, and Divine Love. The same is true if this person appears to you in your contemplative or dream state, you will have these same feelings. Now this is different from emotion in that the feelings you get from the Living Dhunami Master are all from Divine Spirit and are basically Divine Love, which can only be found above the emotional and mental worlds in the pure positive God worlds. Without this Divine Love, the individual claiming to be a Master can guide you no further than the mental area.

Darwin wrote a great deal about this, I believe he listed 32 facets or aspects of a Spiritual Master, but I think we'll try to keep it simple here. The best way to determine if someone is the Living Dhunami

Master is to ask at the Temple Within and wait for the answer. As long as we have a feeling one way or the other of who we want it to be or who we think it should be, we'll have to wait that much longer for an answer, because Divine Spirit can <u>only</u> give us the answer if we are open and receptive to it.

Now I want to say for those of you who are new to the teachings, or haven't had very many spiritual experiences at the Temple Within, do not be discouraged or disheartened. If the answer does not come right away, be patient, for it will come. Some people feel as though they need to know right away, right this second, and that is not the case. If we think about how much time we have on this physical plane, if we take out 2 weeks or 3 weeks even and wait for an answer at the Temple Within for a few moments a day, that's relatively small when we think of the time we are here on this plane. Also, I want to point out that many people will have an experience in the dream state with the Living Dhunami Master and this will be their answer, because it doesn't always come through the Temple Within or the spiritual or contemplative exercises. Sometimes we get our answers in the dream state because we are more relaxed when we are sleeping than when we are contemplating.

I should say that anyone here looking for theatrics or a grand display should get that out of their head. Divine Spirit is a subtle substance, and many experiences are subtle. It must start out that way for the individual to get used to such things, as I explained before when I stated it must be gradual so as not to unbalance the individual. So if we are having a dream state experience and we have recently asked to be shown who the Living Dhunami Master is, then sometimes we will simply see this individual in the dream state. Now I know some of you are thinking, 'I see many people in my dreams.' Well, here's the important part. If this individual standing before you in the dream state is the Living Dhunami Master, he will have Divine Spirit radiating from him and all around him. This is usually seen as a glow; a bright white, yellow, or blue glow. He will also have and give a wonderfully uplifting feeling of Divine Love. If you see a person, or a Being, I should say, in your dream state and you don't feel anything or you feel sort of negatively or like something is not quite right, this individual or Being is not a Spiritual Master and we can demand that they leave our space.

This brings me to another point that needs to be cleared up. If you are doing a spiritual or contemplative exercise and you have a negative feeling or a bad feeling, or feel like something is wrong, stop! You will never have this feeling if a Spiritual Master is present. The Masters of the Dhunami Order all have a great amount of Divine Spirit and Divine Love flowing through them and you will feel it, if you do not then that Being is not a Spiritual Master or Traveler.

Now some people get confused because they have asked a question and they are looking for an answer in their spiritual or contemplative exercise, and then they get a negative feeling. Instead of banishing whatever Being or thought that produced that feeling within the individual, they think it is the answer they have been seeking. Let me use an example to make this very clear, as it is very important. Suppose I was an individual seeking spiritual enlightenment and I had read this book and used some of the techniques and I wanted to know who the Living Dhunami Master is. So I sit down to have a contemplative exercise and I think I have an idea of who it might be, or someone has told me it is this person or that person. So in my contemplation I ask 'is Jimmy Jones the Living Dhunami Master?' and I get a negative feeling, this does not mean Jimmy Jones is not the Living Dhunami Master. It means either I have had a negative thought or feeling within myself about this individual or about something else, or it means a Being is trying to answer my question that is not the Living Dhunami Master or is not a Dhunami Master.

I want to make this very clear and I want people to understand that you will always have a positive feeling, a feeling of Divine Love, joy, and upliftment if it is a true spiritual experience. If it is not, or we don't have a good feeling, we should try to clear ourselves, our minds and

126

our emotions and try again. Or let it be, come back to it later, maybe a day, a few days, or a week. You can ask any sincere chela of the Dhunami teachings and they will tell you, even if they were being told not to do something, or to change their thinking on something, or that what they were doing wasn't necessarily right, that this was all done with a great feeling of Divine Love. No matter what the Dhunami Masters are showing us or telling us it will always be while they are giving us Divine Love with the flow of Divine Spirit. The Masters can't turn this off, it is impossible. So everyone should know that every genuine spiritual experience has the feeling of Divine Love with it, and if it is not there then it is not the Dhunami Masters, it is not a true spiritual experience, and we should quiet ourselves and look again.

Now the Living Dhunami Master is here to gather up those Souls who are eager to reach the heavenly worlds and help them to reach Self-realization, as well as God-realization if they so choose. Now I want to state here that the Master is human even though he is very spiritually advanced, and is the Godman, he is still here in a body, he is still human, he can make mistakes, he can misspeak, and he can forget things. We should never expect the Living Dhunami Master to be perfect because he is human just like every one of you. Only in Soul can we really have any sort of perfection, as man thinks of perfection. The Living Dhunami Master is just like most men, he's had his spiritual lessons to learn, and he's had his jobs, and his girlfriends or what have you. He's had the same daily life as most of us have, he just has a great amount of Divine Spirit flowing through him and he has become adept at working or traveling in his Soul body.

Another thing that should be cleared up here is that everything the Living Dhunami Master does, both here in the physical as well as in the spiritual worlds, is for the benefit of the individual and the good of the whole. Now people have often looked to individuals who may be working with the Living Dhunami Master on the outer, may be helping him with his writing, printing, or distribution of his works. I want to tell you that these individuals in these positions are being given an opportunity and they are being tested, just as any other chela on the spiritual path of Dhunami. And sometimes they pass these tests, and sometimes it takes them a little while, and sometimes they don't pass them at all, just as any other chela in Dhunami.

My point here is this: no matter what the individual is doing, no matter how much responsibility they have, or how much work they are doing or time they are spending with the Living Dhunami Master, this does not mean we can or should look to them for spiritual guidance. We can only look to our initiating Master, the Master who initiated us, and the Living Dhunami Master of the Time for our spiritual guidance. Those people working closely with the Master are being given a great opportunity for spiritual growth, but so is each and every chela who walks and lives this spiritual path. And here's the thing: would you look to a fellow chela who wasn't working in the physical with the Master for spiritual guidance? No, you wouldn't. These individuals working with the Living Dhunami Master are given that opportunity for their own spiritual growth, not for yours, and not for you to look to them for spiritual growth. No one else can guide you but the Living Dhunami Master and the Dhunami Masters of the Dhunami Order if you truly desire Self and God-realization. And really when you consider it, that every individual is being tested and given opportunities, how do you know these individuals are taking advantage of these opportunities or passing these tests as man likes to say?

So my point here is that we are all on the same page no matter where we are developed in the spiritual worlds, no matter our level of initiation, and no matter our physical work or placement. Every individual is being given opportunities by the Living Dhunami Master and every individual struggles, and learns, and may take advantage of these opportunities. The only individual here on this physical plane that can give us any kind of guidance is the Living Dhunami Master. I am sure this has been stated before, perhaps not just like this, but in the same fashion, but I hope those of you reading this are really listening, understanding, and taking to heart what I am saying.

It is so easy to get side-tracked, to get caught in an individual's position or personality or our own image of them in our minds, but if we allow them to guide us or look to them for answers concerning spiritual matters, our own spiritual guidance or spiritual growth, we are doing ourselves a terrible injustice that is unnecessary. So I want to leave you with this thought; always look to the Living Dhunami Master, but more importantly, always look for the Divine Love, because the Divine Love is a part of the Divine Spirit, and Divine Spirit will always lead you to God.

— May the Blessings Be!

Glossary

BALANCE, LAW OF - The stability that lies in the Godhead; all is completely in balance in God's universal body, the principle of unity, of oneness, but in the lower worlds this unity is simulated by the interchange between pairs of opposites.

CHELA (chee-la) - A student, disciple or follower of the Dhunami Teacher; one who has adopted Dhunami as a way of life.

CONSCIOUSNESS - That state of being in which the individual lives daily. Divided into two parts: 1- the phenomenal depends upon the sense organs for its expression; and 2- the transcendental which is independent of the physical senses and works directly with Divine Spirit. The Dhyanic (duh-yahnik) consciousness represents a higher state than either of these, as both are in union with the universal God spiritual essence. Reality of a particular kind of awareness in Man which is independent of the mind's activity.

CONTEMPLATION - In this teaching, it is a spiritual exercise during which the attention is focused upon some definite principle, thought or idea, or upon the Living Dhunami Master of the Time. It differs from meditation in that the definite object of vision gives purpose to the focusing of attention, and is an active action, rather than the passivity of meditation.

DARSHAN - Spiritual realization or enlightenment brought on or caused by the gaze of the Living Dhunami Master on the inner or on the outer.

DARWIN GROSS, SRI - The Living Dhunami Master who received the Rod of Power on October 22nd, 1971 from his predecessor, Sri

Paul Twitchell. Known spiritually as DapRen, (and now as Dapaji), he held the Rod of Power until his translation on March 8th, 2008. Darwin tirelessly and continuously presented his predecessor's teachings with Divine Love and dedication to all chelas. One of the greatest of the Masters in the Order of Dhunami.

DHUNAMI - A direct path to God that teaches how one can become a co-worker with God; also called the Secret Teachings or the narrow way/path.

DHUNAMI SAINTS - Different from a Dhunami Master in these teachings in that they are concerned primarily with the inner worlds working directly with the Soul bodies. They work in a specialized area of the Dhunami teachings, such as healing, working with animals, children, or spiritual protection.

DIALOGUES WITH THE MASTER - A book by Paul Twitchell dictated to him by Rebazar Tarzs, which is now out of print. Original copies, prior to 1983, are still available in used bookstores and on the internet.
DIVINE LOVE - The merciful love with which the SUGMAD looks upon all creation, the Ocean of Love and Mercy, the SUGMAD.

DIVINE SPIRIT - That which flows out of the universal body of the SUGMAD to sustain all the worlds; the Light and the Sound.

ECK VIDYA (Ehk-vee-dyah) - A book written by Sri Paul Twitchell about the Akasha Science of Prophecy; the modus operandi of delving into the past, present and future used by the Dhunami Masters of the Dhunami Order.

FIVE PASSIONS OF THE MIND - Kama (lust), Krodha (anger), Lobha (greed), Moha (attachment), and Ahankar (vanity).

GODMAN (See Living Dhunami Master

GOD-REALIZATION - Void, omnipresent, silent, pure, and strangely peaceful; cannot be apprehended with the physical senses; realization or awareness of the God state, the knowledge of God; attainment of the higher spiritual state of the supernatural life; the uniting of the human and the divine natures.

GOPAL DAS, SRI (Goh-pahl-dahs) - The Living Dhunami Master during the Twelfth Century BC in Egypt who was responsible for introducing licorice for medicinal purposes as well as the duo-decimal system. He is currently the Guardian of the fourth section of the Shariyat-Ki-Sugmad at the Wisdom Temple on the Astral plane.

INITIATIONS - The first step on the path of God via Divine Spirit. The structure upon which the whole foundation of the spiritual works is built; the means by which the sacred forces within the individual are reactivated to increase and confer within Soul the awareness of the supernatural state of life.

INNER MASTER - Light and Sound blended; the highest form of all love; the immortal or changeless part of mankind.

INNER PLANES - The spiritual planes of existence, which are divided into the lower and higher planes. The Physical, Astral, Causal, Mental, Etheric planes are the lower planes, which are the schools of experience for Soul. The higher planes, also called the God Worlds, are the planes from the fifth or Soul plane up to the SUGMAD; the Alakh Lok (ah-lahk lohk), the Alaya Lok (ah-lah-yah lohk), the Hukikat Lok (hoo-kee-kaht lohk), the Agam Lok (ah-gahm lohk), the Anami Lok (ah-nah-mee lohk), the SUGMAD World (soog-mahd), and the SUG-MAD, the Ocean of Love and Mercy.

IT – The Divine Spirit, the Sugmad ITself, the Inner Master. IT can only be called this, because it is above the masculine and feminine principles; meaning beyond the lower worlds of duality.

KAL - The negative manifestation of God through which the power flows to sustain the lower universes whose vibrations are the coarser nature of matter; the creator and lord of the physical worlds.

KARMA - The law of cause and effect, action and reaction, justice, retribution and reward which applies to the lower or psychic worlds; the physical, astral, causal, mental and etheric planes. The law of universal compensation.

LIGHT AND SOUND - Divine Spirit as the manifestation in the lower worlds of the Absolute Supreme Deity, the Sugmad.

LIVING DHUNAMI MASTER - The Vi-Guru, the Godman; the Divine Spirit personified, the true and competent Master who works for the freedom of enslaved Souls, leading them beyond and out of the lower planes of existence into Self-realization. The awakened Soul, transcending time, space and causation, holding the past, present and future in the palms of his hands; appointed to his high position, he is expected to defend the God-power, the works of Dhunami and the chelas who have put their interest and trust in Divine Spirit. All Living Dhunami Masters have descended from the first Living Dhunami Master, Gakko, who came into this world about six million years ago. Some have been married, others are single; they have all served the

Sugmad and Divine Dhun Spirit faithfully, giving their lives to it.

PAUL MARCHÉ, SRI (Pilo Albrasso) - The current Mahanta, the Living Dhunami Master. He is the 973rd in this unbroken line of the Masters of the Vairag. Sri Paul received the Rod of Power on October 22, 2008 succeeding his Master Sri Darwin Gross, carrying on his message and perpetuating his body of works. Sri Paul works in a state of associated consciousness with Sri Peddar Zaskq, while continuing to make Dhunami, the Direct Path to Sugmad available to those who are ready. Sri Paul will assist several individuals into their own Self-Mastery during his tenure, and he will bring his special talents to bear in the presentation of this unique way of life.

PAUL TWITCHELL, SRI
Sri Paul Twitchell is the Mahanta. He was the Living Dhunami Master from 1965 until his translation on September 17th, 1971. Sri Paul Twitchell brought forth the Dhunami way of life to the peoples of the world through his many books, lectures and writings. Sri Paul Twitchell, known spiritually as Peddar Zaskq, trained his successor Sri Darwin Gross, who served as the Living Dhunami Master and led the Dhunami teachings from October 22nd, 1971 until his translation on March 8th, 2008. As the Designated Mahanta and spiritual head of this path, Sri Paul Twitchell brings new life and hope to thousands through the current Living Dhunami Master of the Time, Sri Paul Marché.

REBAZAR TARZS, SRI (rehb-ah-zahr-tahrz) - The Torchbearer of Dhunami in the lower worlds; the spiritual teacher of many Dhunami Masters, including Peddar Zaskq (Paul Twitchell), to whom he handed the Rod of Power in 1965. Rebazar Tarzs has lived in a hut in the Hindu Kush Mountains for well over 500 years, and appears to many as he helps the present Living Dhunami Master of the Time.

SELF-REALIZATION - The entering of Soul into Daswan Dwar, the first plane of the heavenly country, and there beholding Itself as pure Spirit, stripped of all materiality; Soul recognition on the fifth or Atma plane.

SELF-SURRENDER - Submission to the Inner Master in all areas of life both physical and spiritual, devotion to the Divine Spirit; concentrated love for the Master of mind, heart, and will; love of the Master which is greater than anything else; being so completely interested in the Inner Master that nothing else matters.

SHARIYAT-KI-SUGMAD (shah-ree-aht-kee-soog-mahd) - Way of the Eternal; the holy scriptures of Dhunami; a section is located at each of the various temples of Golden Wisdom on the different planes including the Earth world, guarded by a particular Dhunami Master, who is also the preceptor of these sacred writings, which are under him. Chelas of Dhunami are taken in the dream state to study these great scriptures. The first 2 sections of these scriptures were dictated to Paul Twitchell and printed in book form. Original copies, prior to 1983, are still available in used bookstores and on the internet.

SPIRITUAL CONSCIOUSNESS - Truth realized via the awakening of Soul; consciousness of the presence of the SUGMAD, the activity of IT; being aware of and living in closeness with the Divine Spirit.
SPIRITUAL EAR - Also called the Inner Ear; the faculty within by which Soul can hear the Sound Current, the Divine Spirit.

SPIRITUAL EYE - Also called the Inner Eye; known as the Third Eye, the Tenth Door, or as the Spiritual Eye; the window between the physical and spiritual worlds; Tisra Til.

STRANGER BY THE RIVER - A book written by Paul Twitchell. A collection of uplifting, poetic dialogues between Rebazar Tarzs and Peddar Zaskq along the shores of the Jhelum River, which flows through the city of Srinagar in Kashmir. Original copies, prior to 1983, are still available in used bookstores and on the internet.

SUGMAD (soog-mahd) - The formless, all embracing, impersonal, all pervading; the universal spirit, universal life; the Supreme God; infinite Ocean of Love and Mercy. From IT flows all life, all truth, all reality; all wisdom, love and power; all visible lords of all regions are Its manifestations; IT takes many forms in order that Its purposes may be carried out in all creations, but none of them express Its totality.

ADDY MARCHÉ, SRI (Tamaria Alagonia) - The first woman to reach Self-Mastery since Sri Kata Daki over 7,000 years ago. Known spiritually as Tamaria Alagonia, she assists her husband Sri Paul Marché in the current presentation of the Dhunami way of life. A talented writer, Sri Addy has produced a great deal of material on the subject of Dhunami, the direct path to Sugmad. The marvelous balance a woman in Self-Mastery provides for the group consciousness in Dhunami has initiated the Golden Age sub-cycle predicted by Sri Yaubl Sacabi in his dictations to Sri Peddar Zaskq many years ago.

TRUTH - The essence, Divine Spirit, Soul and life of everything that exists or appears to exist, ITself unchangeable and immortal; omniscient, omnipotent, formless, boundless, unapproachable, unchangeable, the source and beginning of life, an unlimited Ocean of Love and Wisdom.

YOU CAN'T TURN BACK - A book by Darwin Gross written in 1985. A brief autobiography by Darwin that includes guidelines to Self-Mas-

tery and happiness. This book is out of print but copies are still available in used bookstores and on the internet.

Some definitions taken from the Eckankar Dictionary, 1973 edition

Made in the USA
Columbia, SC
12 November 2024

46013248R00085